Necessary
Sins

LYNN DARLING

Necessary Sins

a memoir

THE DIAL PRESS

NECESSARY SINS
A Dial Press Book / April 2007

Published by
The Dial Press
A Division of Random House, Inc.
New York, New York

The names of certain characters have been
changed in order to protect their privacy.

Book design by Francesca Belanger

The Dial Press is a registered trademark of Random House, Inc.,
and the colophon is a trademark of Random House, Inc.

Library of Congress Cataloging-in-Publication Data

Darling, Lynn.
Necessary sins : a memoir / Lynn Darling.
p. cm.
ISBN-13: 978-0-385-33606-2 (hardcover)
1. Darling, Lynn. 2. Journalists—United States—Biography. 3. Lescaze, Lee,
1938–1996. I. Title.
PN4874.D3535A3 2007   2006025307
070'.92—dc22
[B]

Printed in the United States of America
Published simultaneously in Canada

www.dialpress.com

10 9 8 7 6 5 4 3 2 1
BVG

For Zoë

Preface

October 1968

ON THE FIFTH FLOOR of Cabot Hall, the freshmen women talk endlessly of sex.

"Losing your virginity is a political act," Penny says.

"You think everything is a political act," observes Cass.

"Everything *is* a political act," says Penny.

"Oh, *fuck* politics," Maeve says. A little thrill runs through the room. The word is still scandalous, brand new, and bright with squalor. In Berkeley recently they arrested a man for writing it on a sign in public. "I'm not making love to make a statement. It's not like it's a social studies experiment."

A brief silence ensues while Maeve's declaration is considered. We sit on the hard mattresses of the bunk beds, curled up like cats among discarded underwear and singular socks, crumpled reading lists and empty album covers. A damp tea bag sits atop the hopeless economics book whose unread chapters will haunt my dreams for years. Already the debris is heaped layer upon layer, like striations of rock reaching back into an ancient geological age. Sometimes I wonder why no one ever tells us to clean it up.

In point of fact, however, Maeve is not making love to anyone, except for Peg none of us is, and the situation has become a bit disturbing, a flaw that needs fixing if we are to be truly a part of the new world being born.

Sex is everywhere—why had I never noticed?—saturating the growing anger in the air, and infiltrating even the Cabot Hall common room where, during the sherry hour, a guest speaker one evening told us that the regular practice of Kegel exercises, which were gradually revealed to our stunned and disbelieving ears to be the rhythmic contraction of the vaginal walls, would enhance our pleasure and that of our partners in the sexual act. The sexual act! Even now it sounded like something exotic and foreign, a custom practiced in a country far away.

Every day brings a bulletin: in the *Harvard Crimson* we read about a Barnard College senior who had been kicked out of school because she was living with her boyfriend. A national magazine columnist called her a whore, but what she was doing seemed pretty tame compared to all the goings-on around us.

Just last week a sophomore who looked exactly like Doris Day had rushed into our room to tell us she had finally done it—she had had sex with two different men in the same day.

She announced her news with the pride of someone who had just been elected to Phi Beta Kappa.

"Do you think being in love with the first person you have sex with is a bad idea?" Cass is asking.

"Absolutely," says Maeve. "The first time should be with someone who is just a friend, so that you don't end up confusing sex with love."

I study these girls, my companions in the foxhole. Each of them deals with the question of her beauty in a different way. Cass is small-boned and slim-hipped, with spectacular breasts encased in tight-fitting sweaters, and long brown hair restrained in modest barrettes. She will be a double major, pre-med and Japanese, but it is not her ambition but her sophistication that impresses me. She once told us that it was her job to select the presents her father gave not only to his wife but to his mistress.

Peg is tall, with broad shoulders and a squarish body. At my old school she would have been plain, but not here, not now: Peg invents her own beauty, just like Janis Joplin. She is hard to read, both open and opaque, her smile a painting that conceals a secret safe.

Penny bristles, red-haired, prickly. She hides her body away, concealing long legs in loose jeans topped with baggy flannel shirts, and pulls her curls back harshly into a ponytail. She wears no makeup, and makes no effort to please. Her father is a famous professor of socioeconomics; they summer on the Vineyard. All of this embarrasses her. I envy Maeve her British accent, the low vibrato of her voice, the amorous colors in which she wreathes herself, smoky violets and dramatic reds. She writes plays and weeps often, mourning a mysterious lost love.

I wonder if I am as vivid to these girls as they are to me. Impossible: sometimes, when I look in a mirror, I'm surprised to see someone there.

"Well, I guess this is it then," my father had said on the day we arrived in Cambridge, just before the start of the fall term. We stood facing each other on the sidewalk in front of Cabot Hall; he had just hauled the last of many suitcases up five flights of stairs. Sentiment embarrassed him, and so he smiled, his face wreathed as usual in an unassailable optimism. He had always believed that things tended to work out for the best—an increasingly dubious assumption in the waning months of 1968.

"Are you sure you don't want me to help you unpack?" my mother asked. For months, ever since the acceptance letter arrived, my great-aunts had been telling her she was crazy to send a sixteen-year-old girl to a school so far away from our northern Virginia suburb. Uncharacteristically, she ignored them, the dream of Harvard stronger than her fear of their disapproval. But now her confidence wobbled. "Aren't you excited?" she asked. Which meant, *please tell me I did the right thing.*

"Come on, Mother, we've got a long drive ahead," said my father as he eased himself behind the steering wheel, already calculating the time it would take to get home. My mother and I tried a quick and awkward embrace; I was distracted by the unfamiliar closeness, the smell of her lipstick and hair spray. She got into the car—my father always bought the same car—a Ford Country Squire station wagon with fake wood paneling and an ample luggage rack. I watched it vanish around the corner, my mother's arm still waving out the window.

Leaving home, leaving home, leaving home, sang the tires as the car made its slow careful way up the highway that morning. And yet it had not occurred to me that the moment would come when I would be living in a place where my parents were not. I had never spent a night away from home without them.

"I think it would be amazing to be in love with the first man you made love to," Astra says. She is a sylph, slender and always in movement like a water plant gently undulating. Her hair is white blond, even her eyebrows. She knows she will be a dancer; I envy her certainty. "It would be a completely transcendental experience, totally spiritual."

The air is thick and hazy. Except for Astra, we are all learning how to smoke. "Actually, I don't think I want it to be all that spiritual," I say, trying to sound worldly and sophisticated. "That's not really the point, is it?"

I have no idea what I'm talking about. Last week I told the only boy who has ever asked me out that he had made a mistake: he must have me confused, I said, with someone else.

"I think being in love probably does make it better," Peg is saying. "The problem is, if you're in love, then you're kind of limited to one person." She takes a drag of her Virginia Slim and sighs, but the combination makes her cough and ruins the effect. I make a mental note.

"That's a problem," says Cass.

But this question of virginity is only the first of many. After that come the real issues. For instance, there is the matter of what kind of sex to have. I know I don't want to have the kind my parents have. My mother believed in good girls, and the virtue of loving just one man. My father is more pragmatic. "Who's going to buy the cow," he likes to say, "if you give away the milk for free?"

On the other hand, "liberated sex" as depicted in the underground press anyway was a little scary: "You gotta fuck your woman so hard she can't stand up," the leader of the White Panther Party had advised, in one of the many leaflets pinned to the trees in Harvard Yard. And then there were the R. Crumb comix, which nearly always featured hairy guys "balling" (an activity which sounded pretty gross) their big assed "chicks" (something I most definitely was not) in all manner of unbecoming positions. It was guerrilla sex, *épater les bourgeois* sex, but somehow it didn't look like much fun for the girl. Did I have to like R. Crumb sex to be a proper revolutionary?

Already I'm afraid that I'm not much of a revolutionary. Deep down, I don't want to have sex because of capitalism or the war. I want to have sex because it promises to be even more fun than smoking dope, because it is the last thing my parents would want me to do, because I want a bridge to burn and a tribe to join. Because sex will make me, in some final and nonnegotiable way, real.

The world is changing so fast now; I am a straw hat in a hurricane. A month ago I wore the clothes my mother had made me, a complete wardrobe, born of the way she imagined college to be in the forties, when she was putting herself through night school. She had folded them all neatly into a big black trunk: the beige corduroy dress and matching coat, perfect for a date to the football game and the party after, the long paisley bathrobe so cozy on those chaste Saturday evenings in the dorm. Heathery cardigan sweaters matched to the same shade of woolen slacks, plaid kilts and soft print blouses with Peter Pan collars, knee socks and penny loafers, and one racy little number, a jumper made of snow-white leather, through which my mother had painfully punched each stitch by hand.

Now they lay in heaps on the closet floor, the hemlines of the skirts all four inches shorter, thanks to Maeve's merciless scissors. Now I wear turtlenecks and blue jeans; blue jeans change everything. I don't tell my mother this when she calls and asks after the clothes as if they were old friends. How do they look? Which is my favorite? The white leather jumper, I tell her, because I know it is the one she is proudest of.

"Oh God, and then there is the question of orgasms," Maeve is saying. "How do you get one? And what kind? At least boys practice on themselves, all that wanking around and wet dreams and whatnot. Why can't girls do that?"

They can, I said. I know.

I found out on a night in late August as a rush of cool air swept through the window, brushing away all the tedium of summer. The moon was full: thankfully, I had not yet read Anaïs Nin to know what a cliché that was. I lay there in the dark, in a four-poster bed with an arching canopy, over which floated a drift of ruffled white cotton — the bed in which I had slept since I was four. My touching was tentative at first, but it wasn't difficult to figure out what worked and what didn't.

Is there anything like the first time you come? To find your body building to something, without knowing what it might be, to be unable to anticipate, and yet to seek release — I wanted to laugh when it was done and announce the news, I wanted to do it again. I don't remember the day I got my driver's license, but I will never forget the night of my first orgasm.

I tell this story into the smoky air, as the autumn wind beats against the glass, and the lights across the Quad begin one by one to wink on. For a moment everyone is silent.

"But that's a clitoral orgasm," Cass says finally. "We're

supposed to have vaginal ones. I'm not sure it counts if it's clitoral."

After school we scattered. Cass became a doctor. Maeve drank and then got sober. Penny discovered she loved women best, and Astra is probably dancing to this day. Peg dropped out after sophomore year, had a baby, and disappeared. The table her grandfather had carved for her from a tree stump, the one she gave to me for safekeeping when she left, has stood ready for her by the door in every place I've ever lived.

But that night Maeve and I lay in our single beds, eyes wide open in the darkened room. Between us stood an upended milk carton that bore a metal desk lamp, a water glass rimed with ashes, and a small bottle of bourbon. We drank only a little; that was all it took then to stop up the fear and deafen the alarm—how will I know when I've gone too far?—going off in my head.

"Maeve?"

"Yes?"

"Do you think when we finally do make love to a boy, everything will be different?"

"Yes," said Maeve. "Everything."

And it was.

The first time—in a basement rec room with a boy as avid and inexperienced as I was—was shattering, joyous, and irrevocable. After it was over, we smiled like lunatics there in the dark, sticky and slick with sweat and blood, a little awkward and self-conscious, absurdly proud.

I put on my clothes—they were unfamiliar to me, as if they belonged to someone else, and so they did. Sex changed me each and every time—even now it does. I drove home alone, eyes grainy with sleep, feeling simple and dumb and happy, connected to every living thing, to the night itself. Slipping back into the darkened house in which my parents slept, even the furniture looked strange.

The decision to make love to that particular boy on that particular night was the very first decision I had ever made on my own. Something unexpected sprang into crazy life, and the radiance of that moment still shines. Now I see that first time for what it was, a casting off into unknown waters, my coming of age.

Sex introduced me to a new self, a sexual self, more visible than I had ever been. Boys noticed. I took huge pleasure in their noticing and in the power it gave me. In making love I found a daring and a confidence I had never known and the kind of happiness that comes from splashing in puddles after a summer rain.

That young woman, who was me and not me, thought of herself as a pirate, living outside the prim limits of respectability. A jezebel, if you will, but very nice once you got to know her. I knew she wasn't quite real—for a long time it didn't matter. I lived in fantasy and present tenses then, so that even my screwups and pratfalls took place in a world in which my actions had no meaning. How could they? Every affair was a movie, an adventure bathed in mythic romance; every seduction conjured up a brand-new way to be.

Sometimes I would think about the men I'd made love to, each in his turn. Some of them loomed large, totems and temple gods, while others were more like the prizes won at amusement parks: a progressive-rock disk jockey in Richmond, Virginia; the faux scion of a Polish count; a marijuana-runner on the North Carolina coast; a fullback–turned SDS organizer turned unsuccessful novelist in California. Desire was a map on which I traced my past, from the major sites to the little roadside attractions.

A loose cannon—that was how a man I knew once described me. I tumbled into bed with married men and single men, with serious men and gawky boys and friends that should have stayed that way. I made love to heroes of my own invention. I tossed off a thousand careless cruelties and paid for them with my own rococo sorrows and self-inflicted wounds. I was, on occasion, unbearably happy. And over the years I wore the emotional nicks and cuts I sustained with the same mixed pride and alarm with which I wore the long ragged slice of white scar tissue that will always be the legacy of my first moment of joy—the day I rode my two-wheeler alone and without permission and came to a spectacular crashing ruin.

The Rocking Chair Theory of Life, my best friend Lisa christened it: experience everything, so that when you are sitting, covered in shawls, on the front porch of the old age home, you will have nothing to regret. The perfect theory for a contingent life, in which each adventure had no connection to the next.

And then I fell in love with a man, and loving him changed everything.

Not simply through the happiness he gave and the good he found in me: this is a love story, not a fairy tale. Within our romance was a reckoning—with what I was willing to do for happiness, the pain I was willing to inflict, the inevitable cost, and the consequences to myself and to others.

He saw me, not my pretense and posturing. I saw him, not the fantasy in which I tried to clothe him. In marriage we found the fragile, endlessly mutating web that connects our angels to our demons, enmeshing us in contradictions, teaching us how not to be afraid of them. Together we wrote a story that made sense of all the others I had ever told myself.

The story ended sooner than it should have, in the long last hours of a summer night, but the bounty it brought, the lessons it taught, are with me still.

Chapter One

THE WHITE HOUSE correspondent for the *Washington
Post* gleamed like a brand-new car.

Even his name was elegant: Lee Adrien Lescaze.

That day he wore a double-breasted gray flannel suit, its
patrician authority both undercut and emphasized by the
burnt-orange shirt with white collar and cuffs, the blue silk tie,
the polished black wingtips. Any other man would have
looked like a dandy, but his ease and confidence dispelled any
such idea. He was no schmo, as my grandmother would say.

He was headed for the newsroom, and as he passed my
desk, he tossed me an amused, detached smile. Something
in me stirred.

I knew about Lescaze—everyone did. He was something
of a legend at the *Washington Post*: an elegant writer, the
quintessential foreign correspondent who had been assigned
first to Vietnam, where his stories about the Tet Offensive
had earned him a reputation for courage and rare insight,

and then to Bangladesh and Hong Kong and many of the world's dangerous and dusty places. In the newsroom he'd worked as both national and foreign editor; his name was on some of the short lists as a possible successor to Ben Bradlee, the editor-in-chief.

His background was glamorous: his father had been a distinguished Swiss-born architect, his mother the locus of a literary and cultural salon for New York artists and intellectuals. He'd gone to Exeter and Harvard—rumor had it he'd smashed up a Jaguar there. He played tennis and squash, spoke Mandarin and French, collected jazz, blues, and rare books—first editions of Samuel Beckett and Ezra Pound. He wrote book reviews with the same finesse as he did war dispatches, and he talked of the Mets and Matisse with equal adoration. He was said to be charming and witty, yet buffered by a nearly opaque reserve. No one claimed to know him very well. To catch the eye of a man like that would be something.

Lescaze hadn't been around the newsroom much—for the last four years he had worked in New York as the paper's bureau chief there, living in the Turtle Bay town house in which he was born, with his wife and three children. Newsroom wisdom had it that assignment had been something of a furlough, easy coasting after time spent on the cross as the national news editor under one of the paper's most notoriously difficult silverbacks. Now he was back in harness, assigned to the White House, and he and his colleagues were in constant motion: Ronald Reagan had won the 1980 election in the sort of landslide that made everyone in official Washington walk a little faster. Careers would be made, while others came undone.

Mine for one, I thought grimly. In the Style section, the math was simple but exacting: the longer the stretch between stories, the more dazzling the next one had to be. I had hardly been in the paper at all lately, and other, fresher bylines were appearing below the most prominent headlines. Patience was wearing thin. The editor of the section wanted to have a little talk with me later that day. This story had to be good.

Style was different from the rest of the paper. It was relatively new then, a gorgeous, bitchy, brilliant feature section that had emerged from what used to be the women's pages, one of the first of its kind. Some of the writers on the national and metro staffs, the real reporters as they thought of themselves, saw Style as a kind of sandbox for the terminally unprofessional, but from the perspective of my own overheated romanticism, it was heaven. After three years the place still dazzled me. A study in the triumph of personality over character, the section nurtured neuroses that would have driven Freud to drink, tolerated egos the size of Cleveland, fetishized obsession, vanity, and genius, and produced some of the best writing I have ever read. Style was steeped in ambition, insecurity, and malice, all of it on display, and all of it, to my fevered ideas of greatness, utterly wonderful.

The editors gave writers a lot of latitude in Style. Temper

tantrums and tears, Proustian eccentricities, expense accounts equaling the GNP of small third-world countries—nothing seemed to matter but the quality of the writing. To keep your balance in a place like that, it helped to have a sense of your own worth. To remember that journalism was just a job and that writing, like baseball, was a matter of batting averages—a hit every third time up was good, amazingly good.

There were older and better writers who tried to tell me these things, but I didn't believe them. No—each story was a judgment, deciding my fate.

I forced myself back to the green letters floating on the black screen. I hated computers: words behaved differently when they hadn't been hammered into the page by metal keys and a satisfying clack. So hard to summon in the first place, they slipped away too easily from this eerie darkness, disappearing like makeup at the end of a long night. Writing was scary enough without that.

If only I could write the way I kissed, then everything would be perfect. Then I would work with courage and abandon, then I would write for the joy of it, I would take the rapids in a bark canoe. I would know how to write the way I knew how to laugh: and I would let the writing come the way laughter does, rushing in on a rising tide.

That day I was writing about a woman who didn't know who she was—autobiography, I realize, but only now.

The woman had appeared on *Good Morning America* the

week before. She sat rigid as a doll, staring straight into the television cameras without blinking her blue-gray eyes. The host, David Hartman, called her Jane, as in Jane Doe. She had been found on a Florida beach naked and dying, her clothes folded neatly by her side, her face frozen in a grinning mask, able to move only her eyes. She could remember nothing about herself, not even her own name.

"I try to remember, and I can't recall where I went to school, if I have any friends," she had said. As she spoke, a phone number trailed across the bottom of the TV screen, the one to call if you had any information about her. "I feel I'm left alone in the world. I'm just trying to go about my life as best I can." A few hours later I was on a plane to Miami.

Since the TV show, hundreds of families had come forward to claim the young woman, saying that she was the one who drove off in the blue Torino two years ago, she was the one who climbed into the car headed for Oregon, the one who walked out the door without saying goodbye. It didn't seem to matter that Jane Doe was a blue-eyed brunette in her early thirties. "Crystal would be almost seventeen years old," one mother wrote. "It is a family trait that during sickness or trauma, the brown eye pigment changes to a blue-gray cast. If you need proof, I will furnish it through further data."

The Fort Lauderdale police chief had a theory about women like Jane Doe. He said it was all the fault of Dr. Spock. In the sixties, he said, "youngsters weren't brought up to respect authority or believe in accountability. They're frightened by it. They can't cope with distasteful reality, so they just pick up and take off."

I met Jane Doe in a small courtyard outside one of the brightly colored concrete bungalows that dotted the campus of the Florida State Hospital, home to nine hundred psychotic and schizophrenic indigent men and women. She had fluffy brown hair and two moles on her pale neck. On TV, the police chief had noted that apart from the moles she had no distinguishing marks, no tattoos or scars or vaccinations. "Jane, you're perfect," the talk show host had said, and in a way she was, swept clean of every mistake she had ever made.

The woman without a memory sat at a table, her hands busy with a piece of pink cloth, her eyes staring straight ahead. "I think I'm lost and wandering around," she said. "I feel ashamed, and I don't know why I feel that way. But I try not to think about that. I think, I'll be busy all morning, and then I think that I'll be busy all afternoon. Everything is so nicely planned for me."

She didn't seem to be in much of a hurry to find out who she was, or whether she belonged to anyone, and I liked her for that.

"I'll be happy, I guess," she said. "I used to be depressed that I would never remember, but now I think maybe my mind knows what's good for me."

It was strangely soothing to be in her presence, perhaps because Jane Doe distilled the confusion in which my friends and I sometimes floundered. Identity was fluid then, unhinged from the past, unconnected to the future, as if we lived in an entirely new tense, the present problematic.

The women I knew improvised, making themselves up as they went along. They careered around corners, sailed off cliffs, went walkabout. Gone was the stately procession of changes that marked their mothers' way: daughter to wife, mother to widow. They left the cadre, left the country, gave up meat. Joined a Zen monastery, the police force, AA. The redhead in San Francisco became the brunette in Paris. The yogi became a bartender. The painter went to law school. There were so many ways to be.

Those of us who attempted more traditional careers hid within a sort of souped-up version of our own personalities, tougher and shinier than we trusted ourselves to be. But the effort was exhausting sometimes. It took so much effort to brandish bravado and hide uncertainty, to exaggerate one's eccentricities and pocket the parts that didn't fit, to make up a character in which to hide, only to find that she threatened to overwhelm the rest. To ricochet between delight that anyone bought the act and a loneliness like no other. "People who have met me only three times are taken in . . . ," wrote Colette. "If I were a man and knew myself profoundly, I wouldn't like myself very much. . . . I say that today, and then tomorrow, I'll find myself charming."

A few days after I got back to Washington, the sad, simple truth about Jane Doe was discovered. She was a former secretary from Minnesota who had drifted down to Lauderdale looking for a new life and found instead a boyfriend who beat her—she had been running away from him when something happened to her on that scruffy patch of beach that sank her memory beyond recall. Her family came to claim her, the mother and father with whom she had cut all ties five years before.

At the press conference, she was asked how it felt to be reunited to her true identity. She hesitated, seemingly ambivalent toward the old and unremarkable reality. She said she thought Jane Doe was a beautiful name.

It was late in the afternoon. The deadline for the first edition, the bulldog, was approaching. Around the corner the metropolitan, foreign, and national editors had begun bellowing for copy, reporters were typing madly while hunched still further into their phones, and the enormous fluorescent newsroom was humming with a distinctly sexual heat and energy, the air dense and heavy the way it is before it rains.

But in Style, where most of the features were edited ahead of time, it was pretty much business as usual. In a nearby cubicle the classical music critic waxed indignant over the pretentions of the latest operatic ingenue. He sputtered into the telephone, outrage illuminating his pink cherub cheeks: "And she calls herself a mezzo! With that puny little cadenza?"

Across the way one of the best and easily the most neurotic writer in the section reached for another paper napkin.

He stuffed it into his mouth and chewed it thoughtfully as he filled a manila file folder with microscopic runes that would eventually morph into a dazzling lede. At the central editing desk the section's canniest political writer heaped invective on the copy editor who had changed a verb without her consent.

More interestingly, the two most glamorous writers on the paper—both of them stylish, smart, and wickedly talented—were standing outside the editor's office exchanging smiles and compliments, the extreme insincerity of which could only mean that a major fight was brewing over who would write the profile of the new White House chief of staff.

By the end of the day I had written nothing worth keeping. I told myself there was still hope of turning in a good story, something more than a patch job. I would work all weekend. I promised myself a quiet evening of chamomile tea, a proper dinner, an early bedtime. I packed up my things as unobtrusively as possible. With luck, I would be able to slip away unnoticed and escape, at least for the moment, that little chat the editor had mentioned.

I'd almost made it to the elevator when I heard Shelby's voice. "Could you stick around?" It wasn't a question.

The editor-writer relationship, like any other intimate intersection of personalities, is essentially a neurotic one. In the newsroom the templates tended toward the classic: predator and prey, dominant-submissive, codependent, victim-perpetrator, or as in my case, parent-child.

The *Washington Post*, my *Washington Post*, was a con-
clave of fathers, powerful, iconic, Zeus-like, to flirt with and
taunt, to prove myself against, to defy and yet to please, always always to please. They brought out the mischief in me,
and they cuffed me when I went too far. They knew where to
draw the line, so I never had to. They were the only ones
who could tell me if I was any good.

Best of all was Bradlee, the man who had shepherded the
paper through the Pentagon Papers and Watergate. Handsome, aristocratic, fascinating, and ruthless in equal measure, he raised the bar high, roaming the newsroom swinging
an imaginary tennis racket, asking his favorite question: what
have you done for me lately?

To waltz uninvited into his office, to beard the lion in his
den, to make him laugh, was exhilarating, scary fun, like
walking into a haunted house. Of course I had a crush on
him, as did many another reporter in the newsroom.

But most important in my immediate world of worship
was Shelby Coffey III.

The assistant managing editor for Style was in his early
thirties then, young for a job of that importance and still boy-
ish in appearance, a good-looking Tennessean who dressed
in an endless supply of rumpled khakis and pastel cotton
button-down shirts whose frayed collars gave him the appearance of a wayward college boy. He had a thatch of un-
ruly black hair, a cadenced drawl, and a charm he wielded
with the deftness of a stiletto. A formidable writer himself, he

had apparently read every work of literature worth reading and brought to good writing the purity of a lover's passion. There was more to him, of course: his own ambition was the vein of iron that underlined the graceful contours of an easy smile; and the anger that coursed when he was crossed ran deep, betrayed only by the throbbing of a small blue vein on his left temple.

In the end he would teach me everything about writing except how to claim it as my own.

Some Style reporters—particularly those who were disciplined, unpretentious, and consistent in their work—considered Shelby manipulative, a consummate courtier to those in power at the *Post*, but he charmed me from the day he gave me my first assignment for Style: a profile of an upper-crust society bandleader. I was fresh from the Metro section, where marching orders rarely went beyond the advice to keep it short and make it sing. I was thinking of the number of inches of copy he wanted when I asked him what he had in mind. "What I'm looking for," he said, "is an elegiac tone poem." As if it were a standard genre for a newspaper, like breaking news or obits.

An admirer of Tom Wolfe, Truman Capote, and the other groundbreaking writers of what was then the New Journalism, Shelby took a literary approach with any writer who was interested, and I was a total sucker for such attention. If I was uncertain about what tack to take in an assignment, he would read me haiku or recommend a book of Barthelme's short stories—anything that might provide a kind of mood music for the effort at hand. Once he suggested that I write a story in stanzas, like Wallace Stevens's "Thirteen Ways of Looking at a Blackbird." I had no idea what he was talking about, but I tried to do it anyway.

To some writers, such suggestions were eccentric at best or even annoying. But I was flattered, finding in the attention a sign that perhaps I wasn't as ordinary as I feared. Shelby gave his writers whatever they wanted: room to move, a place to land, and if you pushed him too hard, the rope to hang yourself.

That evening I walked into Shelby's office and slumped, gracefully I hoped, into the nearest chair.

"From the look on your face, I'm guessing we're not going to be discussing Sei Shonagon's *Pillow Book*," I said, testing the ambient mood.

"That girl could probably teach you a thing or two, missie," he said, smiling.

We had had these talks before but usually at my instigation. I would get depressed and hang around looking sad and weepy until Shelby would finally call me into his office and gently ask what was wrong. But this time it was Shelby who wanted to talk, and this time it was serious.

"So. What's going on with you lately?" he began.

"I think I'm suffering from anomie."

"What do you mean?"

"I'm not sure. I saw it on the back of a Volkswagen—a

vanity plate. According to the dictionary, it's a state of personal unrest, stemming from a lack of purpose or ideals. I see it as one of those vague but chronic conditions that Victorian women always got, like the vapors or neurasthenia."

My effort to amuse was unsuccessful. Shelby moved quickly to the subject at hand: my erratic performance. He subscribed to the eccentric tortured-artist school of writing and tolerated much in its name, but only up to a point. He tried to talk to me about working hard and consistently, about being professional, about building a career. He asked me a question. "What do you want for yourself in the next five years?"

"That sounds like a question from one of those 'ten-ways-to-be-a-perfect-boss' books you read when no one's looking."

"It's still a good question."

I pretended to think about it, then tried to fend him off with a wisecrack. "By then I'd like to have the perfect pair of red slingbacks and a mascara that doesn't run when I cry."

But Shelby said, "I'm serious."

"I guess I've never thought about being alive in five years," I said. "Byron didn't have a five-year plan. Or Kerouac."

"That sounds like pretty lofty company for someone who yesterday was sitting underneath her editor's desk in tears convinced she would never write another good sentence."

"Well, I aim for a carefully calibrated equipoise between overweening arrogance and abject self-hatred."

I was trying for a lofty pretentiousness that would make

him smile, but it was true in its way. I kept a precarious balance in those days, one minute secretly convinced I was a genius, the next embarrassed by what a presumptuous, mediocre nonentity I was.

"I'm afraid," I said finally, "of not being any good. If I don't write, I'll never find out how bad I am."

"If you don't write, you'll never know how good you can be."

I tried to explain. "It's like I'm waiting for something to happen," I said. "For the phone to ring, for the light to turn green, for the ship to sail into the harbor."

"For a chariot to swing low and carry you home?"

"Something like that."

"I think in that case death tends to be something of a pre-requisite."

"Well then, I'll settle for the slingbacks," I said. I could feel the tears welling up.

Shelby smiled, but his eyes remained intent, as if he were trying to gauge whether there was any potential for salvation here. I knew he'd given up, at least for the moment, when he negotiated a graceful surrender. "You know, in some cultures the foot is one of the most eroticized parts of the body. Maybe there's a story here—thirteen ways of looking at a slingback...."

After Shelby left, I walked through the main newsroom, nearly deserted now, on my way to the elevator. The White

House correspondent was sitting at his desk, hanging up the phone.

I had met Lescaze briefly the year before, in New York. I was in the city to attend a press conference, gathering string for a profile of a formerly important person, the kind you are somewhat surprised to find is still alive. He had been at the conference as well and was also planning to write about the formerly important person. Politely, we ceded the story to each other before calling our respective editors to claim it for ourselves. I won—a Pyrrhic victory at best; the consequent story was so boring, I imagined scores of readers falling asleep and landing in their oatmeal when they read it.

I walked over to his desk. He looked quizzical, pleased, uncertain. I could think of no legitimate-sounding excuse for the true nature of my mission, so I finally plunged ahead: "I hope you're not too busy to have lunch with me sometime..."

That was how it began, a small stone skipped on a placid pond, a dare I dared myself.

Chapter Two

MY FAMILY always lived in places where the trees had just been planted. My father was an officer in the army then, assigned to a new post every three or four years. The army provided living quarters, but my mother hated everything about living on base, from the tight-lipped hierarchy among the officers' wives, to the arrogance of the young lieutenants whose job it was to inspect her housecleaning, running their white-gloved hands along the surfaces of her furniture, looking for evidence of dust.

As soon as they could afford it, she chose her own home, my father scouting ahead for possibilities in the new place before we had left the old. Tired and travel weary, we would pull into the tarry driveway of the new house in the brand-new subdivision just a few moments after the paint was dry, when the bare black soil still gave out a sharp scoured smell and bore faint traces of the earth-mover's metal teeth.

I loved it. You could be anyone in a place like that. Back

then I felt sorry for the kids I would meet in each new school, the ones who had lived in the same place all their lives. They had to be who they were, never able to start over, to tell a new story, to become someone else.

But I saw things differently when I got older. My first year out of college I worked on a weekly newspaper in Richmond, Virginia, founded by a classmate of mine, a native son. When I arrived he took me on a tour, driving me down broad avenues over which statues of the fallen sons of the South still stood guard, past old houses belonging to even older families. He showed me other landmarks as well: the Episcopal church where his family had occupied the same pew for generations, the school where he had suffered his boyhood torments, the country club where he had cut down the flag when the membership refused to lower it the day Martin Luther King was killed. Fury mixed with a reluctant loyalty as he told his stories; all he had ever wanted was to leave, yet the city drew him back. For the first time I felt a stab of envy for someone so rooted to a place. To know where he had been, I thought, must tell him so much about who he was now, how far afield he might have wandered for better or worse.

Prosperity Avenue in Fairfax, the road that led from the highway to the street where my parents now lived, held no such memories for me—my family had moved into the neighborhood after I had left for Harvard. It had never been my home, just a stage on which to twirl my grown-up self when I came for a Sunday-night dinner.

Still I always found comfort in the shade trees that arched overhead all along the way to their house. They were, for me, as they were for my mother, a proof of a settled success. Now, driving past them at this oddly early hour, I felt like a trespasser, stealing an unmerited solace from their cool green light.

The evening after my talk with Shelby had betrayed me. I had planned on a modest glass of wine taken in chaste solitude, a virtuous restraint ensuring an early morning and a fresh start on my as yet incoherent story. But then the phone rang—*What are you doing tonight?*—and the wrong me answered, the one who always said yes when she should have said no. I would go out for just a little while, I promised myself, but the night expanded to include a ragtag collection of people—a pair of junior White House staff members, a bar owner, a California grower of hydroponic grass, a Style assignment editor—and a succession of condiments, legal and otherwise. By the time I returned, the hours of the night had disappeared and a dull gray light had infiltrated my bedroom and rendered the lamplight superfluous.

I tried to sleep, but the crows of anxiety and craving had begun to dig sharp claws into my shoulders, and a hectoring furious voice set in, reminding me of all the work that would not get done that day, scolding me for once again figuring out a way to shoot myself in the foot. There was only one way to shut up that voice, and that was to outrun it.

The George Washington Parkway was not the fastest or the most direct route to my parents' house, but at seven o'clock on a Saturday morning it was empty and quiet. It was my father's favored route. Like him, I preferred its graceful uninterrupted curves to the stoplight-studded frustration of Arlington Boulevard. But mostly I took it because he did.

The light wobbled as I drove, and the hum of the car engine scraped across my brain. Sometimes I almost enjoyed a hangover; some of them were quite modest in their demands, entailing only a sleepy afternoon on the sofa reading P. G. Wodehouse and eating Hostess cupcakes. Others had a lovely rueful quality that yielded without protest to a Bloody Mary and left behind a vague feeling of cosmopolitan sophistication, like that emanating from Nick and Nora in the *Thin Man* movies. Even a brainblaster, the kind that stripped away most of the will to live, had its good points, leading sometimes to a Zen-like state of perfect egolessness or, failing that, to a sensuousness that guaranteed outstanding sex.

But the hangover that morning was not so merciful. It was a gigantic Jonathan Edwards sinners-in-the-hands-of-an-angry-God hangover, the kind that demanded immediate placation if it were not to expose me as the mess of a girl I really was.

I began the well-worn rosary of fault, which ranged from last night's failure of discipline to the lack of vegetables in my diet. Looking back, I'm amazed at the amount of guilt and self-loathing in which my friends and I indulged, but I understand now why it was so necessary. There was a peculiar pleasure to be had in the act of bottoming out. Shearing myself of absolutely any claim to goodness or self congratulation left me free to start again, shining again with promise and purpose.

I would change, I told myself that morning, as I always did on such occasions. There was still time. After all, I wouldn't be an absolute certified failure until I was thirty. I still had a year or two in which to become an entirely different person. I would stop smoking. Again. And start running. Again. I would work hard, get organized, pick up my clothes. I would never, ever procrastinate.

By the time the Mustang skimmed off the Beltway at the Fairfax County exit, a vision had formed, one that let me breathe again. There I was, the new me, in all my future radiance—glowing with fitness in a pair of sexy red satin running shorts, cooking soup in my spotless kitchen. In this vision, the phone rings. I answer it. Oh my goodness, mirabile dictu! I've won the Pulitzer Prize!

Piece of cake.

I turned right onto my parents' street and turned off the engine; I loved coasting down the street with just enough momentum at the end to pull into the driveway—it was the same satisfaction you get from peeling an orange in just one curvilinear strip. I checked my face in the rearview mirror for signs of fatigue: for the most part they lay buried beneath a little blush and a half-pound of concealer. Then I tried out a smile: a glassy-eyed scarecrow grinned back. Retreat! Retreat! This visit was a terrible idea. I was too pale, and my hands were too shaky, the sun was too bright. I couldn't possibly pull this off.

I walked through the front doorway without knocking, to find them where I knew they would be, sitting around the kitchen table — my father, my mother, and my grandmother. The table was small and round, its shiny veneered surface covered up by faded flower place mats. The place mats were lumpy — underneath them were bills to be paid, scraps of paper bearing phone numbers scribbled in haste, a spare needle or two, and addresses torn from Christmas card envelopes: my mother's filing system. An ancient sewing machine dominated the table, pushed only slightly to the side to make room for the coffee cups.

They were surprised to see me so early in the day. I told them I'd been up all night, talking to friends; I did not tell them how I managed that. I loved having a secret life, something that was only mine, imagining myself a spy in the grown-up world of rectitude.

"Up all night, and you couldn't tell by looking at her," said my mother. "If I did that, I'd look like something the cat dragged in."

Both my parents stood up as soon as I sat down, my mother in search of a chore that needed doing, my father to begin making breakfast. They were nervous around me now. Who could blame them? I had worked so hard to create the distance between us.

Kill your parents. That's what the Yippies said when I was in college. An incendiary phrase for an incendiary decade, but nothing more, really, than a harsh restatement of a task required of every generation in confronting its elders. Even then I had winced at the wording but I knew what they meant: Kill the part of yourself that obeyed their rules. Kill the limits they placed, and kill their plans, kill the dreams they fashioned for you out of those they themselves had had.

Now I see those dreams in a different light. But back then I mistook their fierce hopes for the future, the relentless imperative to improve to mean that their love for me was negotiable, contingent on my success. I think I began to hate the girl they wanted me to be, as if she was the favored child and I the changeling.

And so I tried hard in college to ditch that girl, her complaisance, her endless desire to please. I changed everything I could about myself and then I girded myself for their resistance and their rage. But there was none — only bewilderment and worry. I couldn't understand then why they let me strike out at them. I didn't understand until I had a child of my own.

When Zoë was about four or five, she was given a book of folktales from around the world. It was one of those self-consciously liberal books designed to produce tolerant children. India was represented by the story of Buddha and the tigers. One day Buddha is walking along when suddenly he is confronted by a mother tiger and her cubs. The mother is starving and too weak to attack him. Buddha could walk away and save himself. Instead he throws himself off the cliff so that the tiger and her cubs will live.

What's that about? said Zoë.

It's about what parents do when their children turn into tigers, I said.

Will I turn into a tiger?

Maybe.

I hope I'm a big one.

My mother grabbed a battered gray dishrag from the kitchen sink and wiped the floor. She wiped it the way every woman in her family did—bending from her waist, legs planted far apart, her hips high in the air. Her people had done it that way from Poland to Pittsburgh; it was as close as we came to a family heirloom.

My father began to crack eggs, melt butter, measure flour. He was a New Hampshire man, tall and straight, the kind who didn't talk much, who poured his love into the things he could do for us. Until I married, he painted every apartment I ever lived in.

My grandmother did not get up. She sat as if welded to her chair in a thin blue nightgown, her hair tight to her head in curlers. Her fine-boned face, riven with lines cut by a lack of money and a lack of joy I could only guess at, still contained a granite beauty. She had no mask, I thought to myself. She wore the face that life had carved for her. Her blue eyes contained none of the anxious desire to please I saw in my mother's and in my own.

She looked me up and down. "You keep yourself up," my grandmother said. "You haven't let yourself go, that's good." And then: "You're too skinny. But you're always too skinny."

She appraised me coolly, checking for dents and scratches. She had been one of twelve children born to an immigrant mother and a father so bitterly remembered that for years I thought his name was Dirty Rotten Whoremaster — when I was little, I longed to meet him. She left home at twelve to escape his abuse and went to work in a glass factory. She married and had three children. Her husband worked in one of the city's great steel mills, and she cleaned office buildings — at night, so the neighbors wouldn't know.

She wouldn't talk about the past, even when in my working-class-revolutionary phase I tried to extract from her a parable of class struggle. Why would anyone want to remember such misery? she said. In her house in Pittsburgh she lived in the basement, washing her clothes in a big iron tub, doing the dishes in the sink despite the presence of a washing machine and a dishwasher in the kitchen upstairs. She liked things to stay pristine, unused. The living room furniture was covered in plastic. (In my mother's house the good sofa was covered with a sheet. It was as if my family's faith in the future could be measured in each generation's increased daring where good furniture was concerned.)

She wanted her grandchildren similarly untouched by the damage the world could do. Years later, when I was pregnant, she refused to see me. She didn't want to think of me like that, she said, knocked up, disfigured.

I had dressed up for the visit: a blue corduroy dress with a full skirt, a flowered scarf at my neck, stockings. I wanted to look nice for my grandmother, and I was hoping the change of clothes might bring me closer to the earth's gravitational pull.

"I made that dress, Mother," my own mother said.

"Sure, Dorothy, I know, I know." Her harsh voice was tight with her refusal to cough up the compliment her daughter was soliciting. My mother is a formidable woman, who raised three children, and for twenty years taught world history, geography and psychology at a variety of high schools, but still she lived for her mother's approval, just as I lived for hers no matter how much I tried not to. We were like the skittish little dogs you see at the circus, each on his hind legs begging for attention from the next one up the ladder.

"Look at the tailoring," my mother says, pulling up my skirt as if it were hanging on a mannequin. "You don't know how hard it was to get it like that, I was copying a Ralph Lauren dress I saw in Lord and Taylor."

"How much was that material?" my grandmother asked.

My mother told her. "That's ridikalus," said my grandmother. "You got to be some kind of fool to pay that kind of
money."

The smell of bacon filled the air, and a wave of nausea
hit me. About the only thing I could possibly eat was the cel-
ery stalk in a Bloody Mary.

"How are things at the *Post?*" my mother asked. "I
haven't seen your name in the paper lately. People are asking if you still work there."

"I wish you wouldn't ask me questions like that," I said
indignantly, ignoring the inconvenient fact that it was exactly the same question Shelby had asked the night before.
"You don't understand. Writing is really, really hard. It's not
like I'm making tin cans. Sometimes I can't eat or sleep, it
makes me so crazy."

"But if it's so hard," my mother asked, "why do you do it?
Why don't you get a job that you enjoy?"

"Because writing makes me happy," I yelled. "Can't you
see that?" My mother flinched at the anger in my voice.

My father hated conflict and would do anything to stop a
fight. He stepped in, grabbing the first distraction he could
think of. "Dorothy, have you seen the cast-iron skillet?"
Probably not the best choice, since the skillet was sitting on
the counter right behind him.

My mother, stung by my irritation, turned it on my father. She began to yell about how stupid he was, which
made me anxious. Not coming-down anxious, just plain old

Mommy-and-Daddy-are-fighting anxious, which launched me finally into the stories they wanted to hear.

"Actually, Ben Bradlee complimented me on the story I was working on," I said quickly. It was kind of true—I'd had a daydream where Ben would love my story so much, he would put it on the front page. After I'd written it, of course.

"Really? What did he say?"

I told them something Bradlee probably would have said to someone, including all the profanity he would have used, thereby titillating my mother and amusing my father. I wasn't formless anymore, no longer exposed. I was becoming once again the girl they were proud of.

I could tell myself I was doing it for them, but it wasn't entirely true—I needed to be that girl again, if only for a morning.

I told more stories—about how one of the stars in the Style section had complimented a dress my mom had made for me, and the way I'd flirted with some policeman to get a small scoop about a recent murder—until everyone was re-assured and I was bathed in their pride.

I watched my parents watching me. My mother beamed, my grandmother listened, unblinking. I saw my old self taking shape in their eyes, the one who went to Harvard and got a great job, the one who made it to the next rung of the ladder, the one who redeemed the old slights of poverty and class and the implacable hunger for something better.

Everyone has a drug of choice, a way out of the ordinary,

a mirror in which you always look better than you know yourself to be. For some it's sex; for others, alcohol or religion, or art, or even drugs themselves. Mine was transgression or so I liked to think. My parents had a drug too: I was their drug.

My father served me up an epic breakfast, a song of love, a magic charm. He had to search the topmost cupboard shelf for a platter big enough for it all, for the eggs fried in butter and the bacon, the pancakes with maple syrup, the sliced tomatoes, the leftover spaghetti, even a bit of steak. He used to make such breakfasts on weekends sometimes, and I would try to rise to the challenge and eat every bit. Suddenly I was stupendously hungry. Rocked by waves of anxiety and exhaustion, I clambered onto this fragile raft constructed of their love and concern. Soon enough I would kick it away, making for the uneasy frontier where I now lived, but for the moment it was home.

When I was young, my favorite show was *I Love Lucy*. The episode I loved most was the one in which Lucy tries to get Ricky some much-needed publicity by impersonating the Maharincess of Franistan, fictional royalty from a distant and completely fabricated country.

Unlike most of Lucy's schemes, this one is relatively successful. She convinces the press that the Maharincess has come all the way to New York just to hear Ricky sing. She arrives in disguise at the Tropicana, answers questions from obsequious reporters, and behaves imperiously toward all who approach her. She listens entranced as Ricky sings twenty-five songs to her, every other one the bongo-bashing "Babaloo." Everyone is deceived, even her husband.

How wonderful, I thought every time I watched it: to stand next to the people who knew you best and hide yourself completely. To be simultaneously secret and exposed, to be concealed in plain sight, to keep yourself safe and to deliberately risk that safety.

Still, there are limits to any masquerade, a point where the hard rock of self finally pokes through the thin stuff of disguise. Ricky finally figures out what's going on when he realizes that his wife is the only person on the planet who would listen to that much "Babaloo." He wasn't angry as he often was in the aftermath of Lucy's schemes, he was touched.

At the time I thought the best part of the episode was Lucy's disguise, and the fact that she finally got away with something. It's still my favorite—now, though, it is the ending I like, the fact that it is love that finally exposes her and that, once exposed, she is still loved.

Chapter Three

"My Tho still smells of death. Most of the bodies—Vietcong and friendly—have been removed from the streets, but some remain. In the wreckage of their homes, people are looking for things to save."

—Lee Lescaze
Washington Post
February 1968

"Destroying is a wonderfully exhilarating thing to do. It is mischievous and healthy. It moves the spirit and the soul. It is direct, concrete and eternal."

—*Harvard Crimson*
October 1968

MY LUNCH with Lescaze (as I thought of him then) took a week to arrange, delayed by the inconvenient intrusion of presidential press conferences and breaking news.

Finally, though, we sat across from each other at a rickety table in the café across the street in the Madison Hotel, a place to which *Post* reporters often repaired to share information or more often gossip.

He was late to that first lunch and flushed after his hurried walk from the White House. His FBI clearance still dangled from the metal cord around his neck as he took his seat. He apologized for keeping me waiting but not in the standard insincere Washington way. This man really did think it rude to keep another person waiting.

I studied him while pretending to consider the menu. His face revealed hints of intriguing contradictions. The large tortoiseshell glasses, the high wide forehead, confirmed the intellectual, but the flare of his nostrils, the birdwing curve of his upper lip betrayed, unexpectedly, the sensualist.

He looked up and caught me staring at him. His eyes were hazel. He cocked his head, raised an eyebrow. *What are we doing here?* his expression asked, and I smiled and shrugged my shoulders, suddenly not so sure I knew the answer.

"I've been out of the newsroom much of the time you've been here," he said. There was a slight tremor in his voice. *He's uneasy*, I thought, touched by the idea that such a thing was possible. "You used to be in Metro, right?" he said. "How did you get to Style?"

"Oh, the usual way," I said. "Backstabbing, bribery, sleeping with the editor."

He looked alarmed for a beat—dear god, I thought, apparently he's heard enough about me to make my explanation plausible. But then he smiled, and I relaxed.

"Well, maybe that wasn't it exactly," I said. "I think they just got fed up with me in Metro. The copy editors react badly when you tell them that the changes they're making are ruining the cadence of your sentences."

"You said that? To Brady?" He looked impressed.

He asked me what I thought of Style.

"It's a writhing pit of scandalously indulged show-offs and neurotics," I said. "You know, paradise."

He laughed, taking full advantage of the moment, as if there were not enough of them.

My story on Jane Doe had come out that morning, splashed all over the front of Style. I waited for him to mention it, to tell me how great it was. But he said nothing.

"In fact, I have a piece in today," I finally said, before I could stop myself.

"Yes. I read it." He complimented me in a de rigueur fashion.

"That was enthusiastic," I said. "Now tell me what you really think. I'd like to know."

"It was fine. Perhaps a little long." Later it would become a joke with us; that weak word *fine* was as close as he would come to criticism. But this time he responded to the disappointment in my eyes.

"Not to worry," he said kindly. "Bradlee once told me you were the best writer on the paper."

I beamed, trying and utterly failing to contain my glee.

"On the other hand, Bradlee says that about a lot of people," he said, waiting for a reaction. "He even said it to me." And I laughed at the way he had thrown me off balance.

Politely he asked me what I thought about Jane Doe, and I tried to come up with something that was true but was also a little dramatic, to show him how cool I was. "I envied her," I said. "What a wonderful thing, to walk away from your past." I waited for him to register an expression that proved he found me impressively deep.

Instead he said, "You're very young, aren't you?"

"Not really. I'm twenty-nine. How old are you?"

"I'm forty-two."

"Wow, that's old."

"Thanks."

"But you don't think it's possible? To walk away, I mean? From everything?"

"It's not that easy," he said. "Of course, amnesia probably helps."

The talk turned to the incoming administration. He had a dry, detached humor with which he mercilessly skewered the self-aggrandizement of the new lords of the realm. "He had to say very little," one of his foreign correspondents would say of him years later. "He could eviscerate someone with two words and a well-placed eyebrow. And yet it was never mean or small-minded—more like a private insightful joke on the powers that be, one that you felt privileged to be let in on."

It was the beginning of January 1981. The transition period was nearly over, and Reagan's inauguration was imminent. Lescaze grimaced at the thought of the relentless hoopla he would inevitably witness. Would I be covering the Inaugural Ball?

I flushed. An inaugural ball was a grand exhibition of power, pride, and human vanity on a spectacular scale, just the sort of story the Style section reveled in. But besides the main event, and very much in its shadow, were dozens of satellite celebrations. I'd been appointed to the inaugural equivalent of Pluto, interviewing minor campaign contributors from insignificant states, probably in some VFW hall in the outer suburbs. One of the newest arrivals to the Style section, a beautiful, talented young redhead with the work ethic of a Calvinist preacher, would cover the most important one. And even though I hated covering politics and parties and this was the worst of both, I was ashamed.

"Not really," I said. "Just one of the small ones." I named the girl who would cover the main event.

"She's terrific," he said fervently.

"Yes, isn't she?" I said. "Of course, now that I know you think so, she will have to be killed."

"You remind me of a character in a book I'm reading," he said. "She's glib and brittle, like you."

"She sounds awful," I said. "She'd better be wildly beautiful."

He laughed and called for the check. When I stood up, he helped me on with my coat, and I made a mess of the business, turning into a tangle of elbows and missed sleeves. I'd never mastered backing into an outer garment gracefully. It wasn't a skill that I much needed with men my own age.

After work that day I stopped at a bookstore in Dupont Circle and scanned the book Lescaze had mentioned, *Parade's End*, a tetralogy by Ford Madox Ford. I was looking for a description of the character to whom he had compared me. There she was, one Valentine Wannop, on page sixty-six: "A fair young woman with a fixed scowl . . . She had a short skirt and was panting a little . . . She seemed a perfectly negligible girl except for the frown: her eyes blue, her hair no doubt fair under a white canvas hat. She had a striped cotton blouse, but her fawn tweed skirt was well hung."

How flattering. I bought the book anyway.

In the days after that first lunch, I looked for him in the newsroom, but he wasn't around much, and when he was, he was always far away, on the other side of that enormous space where the big stories, national and foreign, brewed and bubbled. He never looked harried or busy in that self-important way some reporters—including, I'm afraid, this one—did. Nothing false, nothing unnecessary, in his gestures, his speech, his attitude, and yet he knew how to charm—there was a musical quality to his movements and his expressions, to the tilt of his head and the graceful conduct of his hands as he talked to a colleague or an editor. He radiated a subtle fineness. I found it hard to look away.

He still smiled when he passed my desk, but he didn't suggest a second meeting. I was disappointed but not surprised. We came from different worlds.

From a distance, in the newsroom, Lescaze looked like a particularly polished example of the standard-issue *Wash Post* WASP, the men for whom the gates to prep school and the Ivy League had always swung open, who waltzed without a stumble from debutante balls to decorous brides. At the office they wore crisp striped shirts with French cuffs and white collars, the sleeves of which they often rolled up as deadlines neared. On the weekend, they wore their tennis whites as gracefully as they did their tuxedoes. At dinner parties they deployed their cleverness in the service of ambitions no less serious for all their subtlety.

Their rarefied backgrounds did not preclude a work ethic as ferocious as that of the brilliant self-made men from the big state universities. A few months after I started work at the paper, I went out for an uncharacteristic run through Rock Creek Park. After twenty minutes, I hit the sidewalk half dead and filled with virtuous self-congratulation. Walking home, I passed the house of one of the national reporters, handsome, wealthy, Harvard educated. He was standing at his front gate, dressed, as always, in an impeccably cut wool suit. He had been watching me. "How far did you go?" he asked. I told him. "You quit too soon," he said. "You should have run all the way home." He looked at me scornfully, as if because of me, Yale would win the big game or we'd lose Latin America to the Communists or quite possibly both.

I came to work at the *Washington Post* in 1975, a twenty-three-year-old with a one-paragraph résumé, so inexperienced the editors placed me on an extra-long probation. My being there at all, as some of the men in the newsroom made haste to assure me, was the result of a successful affirmative action suit filed by the paper's female reporters; the court's decision had sent the management scrambling for recruits of the requisite gender.

The paper was brilliant then and at the height of its cachet. The Watergate scandal was still heavy in the air. If I had been hired just a few months earlier, I would have seen Robert Redford there, learning how to work the phones in preparation for his role in *All the President's Men*. At the time Woodward and Bernstein still worked in the newsroom, and you could see them—or the tops of their heads anyway—bent over their typewriters and their phones like all the others.

The very air was charged with an intense and feral energy. It radiated from the foreign correspondents, just back from Dacca or Beirut, and from the Pulitzer Prize–winning national reporters, who'd taken their lumps at Selma and been there when Bobby died, as some of them were sure to tell you over lunch or drinks at the bar on the roof of the Willard Hotel, not far from the White House. But it was there too, that same hunger, in the kid working second-string night police. What were they hungry for, these people? And when did they quit? They never quit.

The younger women at the paper shared a different kind of camaraderie.

The fifth-floor women's room was a haven for the desperate and the insecure. There was always someone sloshing gallons of cold water on her face to get her brain to function, or rushing to pee after holding it in for six hours because she was too scared to leave her desk on deadline, or wiping off the mascara that had run when her editor reduced her to tears.

A few minutes after I had written my very first story for the paper, a four-inch epic on a local teenage tennis tournament, I found myself queasy with the effort and weak with relief and slipped off to the bathroom for some privacy.

I crouched in front of a toilet waiting to be sick. Nothing came, just dry heaves and gagging sounds.

"I hate it when that happens," said a delicate girl who was reputed to be one of the best of the interns in the Style section. "It feels so much better when something actually comes up." She said she threw up after every story she wrote. "How about you?"

"I don't know," I said. "I just wrote my first story."

"Hey, that's great!" she said. I thought she looked at me a little differently then, like we were comrades, like she was welcoming me to the neighborhood. "How does it feel?"

"It feels better than anything in the world," I heard myself say. And to my surprise, I meant it.

"Then don't worry. You'll be fine." She was pretty, thin, and tall, with frizzy brown hair and haunting gray eyes. I saw her looking me over as we both gave ourselves a last appraising gaze in the mirror. "By the way," she said as she pushed the door wide open, "in case anyone hasn't told you yet, stay away from"—she named a legendary reporter. "When he gets writer's block, he'll fuck anything that moves."

Young women have two jobs, Simone de Beauvoir wrote. One is to be female, the other is to be human. A second self makes the first job easier, protecting the shaky, unreliable creature developing within. Women fashion them from whatever template the times have to offer: Gibson girl, flapper, the Angel in the House, the devil in a blue dress, the girl with kaleidoscope eyes. I had begun my second self in college, choosing my persona with more deliberation than I chose my major. I was lured by the romance of self-destruction and imminent apocalypse, and my icons were androgynous and enigmatic—Jagger's mocking midnight rambler, Bogart's ruined romantic. I wanted to be intimidating, powerful, desirable, and tragic. I assumed I would die young. I wanted lovers who were, in some ineffable and undefined way, dangerous in the way I wished I was.

After five years at the *Post*, my persona had changed in terms of detail and nuance but remained the same in essence. She was a tatterdemalion creature composed of bits and pieces of old rock songs and half-remembered lyrics: hard-drinking, fast-driving, lawless, and irresponsible. A flirt, who used her sexuality as a counterweight to her professional inexperience and her grave self-doubt.

She was meant to be a temp, someone to get me through the business of being a woman while I figured out what that meant. But by the time I met Lescaze, the character I built for myself had become both my armor and my enemy, protecting me, preventing me, from any formidable encounter with what might lie beneath.

The first book in the Parade's End trilogy, *Some Do Not . . .* is the story of Christopher Tietjens, an upper-crust British intellectual whose world is being smashed to pieces by World War I. Tietjens is a brilliant, stuffy stoic, misunderstood and persecuted by a wife who can't stand him. Gossip mistakenly assumes a romantic liaison between him and the absurdly named Miss Wannop, a radical suffragette who has been caught in the act of defiling an upper-crust golf course.

Tietjens helps her get away from the police, and a wary, erotically charged friendship ensues. They argue about everything from votes for women — "I approve entirely of your methods but your aims are idiotic," Tietjens tells her — to the correct Latin pronunciation of an obscure species of bird.

They are obviously perfect for each other, but Tietjens hesitates through hundreds of pages, unable to square desire with duty. Valentine, one gets the impression, is not similarly burdened.

I read the book compulsively, even at my desk in Style. It wasn't long before I had a crush on the main character. I loved his duality — the passion that played beneath the rectitude, the self-containment that coexisted with a yearning for personal transcendence. And I loved the way he loved Valentine, the way he valued even her awkwardness.

Late one bleak afternoon in February I ducked downstairs to the *Post* cafeteria, trying to avoid assignment to an embassy reception that would almost certainly be chock-a-block with power brokers I would not recognize, discussing policy issues I hadn't heard of. Before long I was deep into Tietjens's latest ruminations about Valentine. She was, he thought, "a little pronounced in manner sometimes, faulty in reasoning naturally, but quite intelligent, with a touch of wrong accent now and then."

"So how do you like it?"

I looked up. It was Lescaze.

"It's interesting," I said lamely, as I scrambled for something to say. "Ah, maybe we could talk about it over lunch sometime."

"I don't usually have time in the afternoon," he said. And then, "What about a drink after work?"

I was surprised. Drinks constituted an entirely different level of intimacy. White House correspondents had drinks with friends and co-workers, but I was neither. There was one possible reason for his invitation, the one that would have been foremost in my mind, but I skittered away from that one as completely implausible.

We met in yet another hotel café, this one considerably downscale from the Madison, well lit and charmless, as if to underscore the innocence of the encounter. He ordered a martini—Bombay gin on the rocks with an olive, very dry. I ordered the same. I'd never had one before—I drank Jack Daniel's mostly, because it was indecorous and ungirly and because I liked the way it burned its way down to a warm interior glow. The first drink was quickly followed by a second. He liked to drink, and he could drink a lot. His thirst seemed to be as deep as mine. Deeper.

A colleague walked by and threw us an appraising look. "I'm going to ruin your reputation," I said lightly, curious to see his reaction. He shrugged. "Ain't misbehavin'." When he saw me look puzzled, he came to my rescue. "It's the title of a Fats Waller tune," he said. "As I'm sure you know." I would always love that about him, how he hated to parade his nearly encyclopedic command of a given subject, or to embarrass someone who might know less. He would need the phrase many times throughout our life together.

"Oh! I see. Well, I'd love to kiss you but your feet's too big," I said.

He blushed a little, and I scrambled to clarify. I wasn't trying to suggest anything—was I? "It's the only Fats Waller song I know," I said hastily. "An old friend used to sing it to me. Because my feet really are very large, huge really, like gunboats." Oh lovely, I thought, that's a charming image. I looked down at his beautiful sculptured hands, the long tapered fingers. The wide smooth band of his wedding ring caught the light. If I ever get married, I thought to myself, that is the sort of ring I would want.

He changed the subject to Valentine and Tietjens and the dilemma they faced.

"Jesus, what is their problem?" I said. "I thought everyone in the British upper class fucked like bunnies."

"You're not sympathetic to their ambivalence."

"Ambivalence I would understand. But this is pathological. Why doesn't he just throw her down on the bed? He's got the perfect excuse—he's about to go to war. He could be killed the next day. Surely sex with Valentine beats gangrene in the trenches. In the sixties we used imminent apocalyse to justify pretty much anything."

"So you think he should forget his own sense of honor and responsibility and ignore his misgivings?"

"It's always worked for me."

"So that would be a yes?"

"No. That would be, if anything, a really good reason not to."

Over the next few weeks, in late February and early March, we met for drinks several times. The invitations on both sides were always offhand, spur of the moment, as if the idea had just occurred to whoever was doing the inviting, which in my case was patently untrue.

I loved our conversations, the volley of black-humored observations and literary references. He was cool to look at, to play against. His charm played beneath the surface of his features, appearing in the briefest of smiles before disappearing once more into deeper waters. I was drawn to the banked emotion I sensed but would not see until later.

I liked the way he laughed at me, at my sense of melodrama. He was amused at my neurotic approach to writing, just as I was amazed by the offhand confidence of his. In Vietnam, he would pour himself a drink and write his copy for the day—after the last round of parties in Saigon, after the last round of mortar fire in the field.

His humor was dark, wry, worldly. Again and again, that is the word I come back to—he was intrigued by the world, its degradation and splendor, the opium dens of Laos, the slums of Soweto, the sinuous allure of Venice. He waded into the largeness of life, and that fascinated me. I lived in an interior world of intense, often murky, self-definition. It was only later that I saw the symmetry between us. Our explorations, one convex, the other concave, comprised a whole.

Lee's impatient disdain for the machinations of the powerful was real, but so was his admiration for their antithesis: the everyday courage and kindness of ordinary people. And he found it everywhere: Saigon, New York City, Accra, Benin, Burkina Faso.

He never made a display of his own kindness, and yet the unstinting testimonies poured forth in the condolence letters, from the freelancers whose fledgling careers he nurtured, to the refugees from Pakistan and Saigon for whom he found homes and jobs.

"Ouagadougou revives my contact with the types who give large chunks of their lives to relief work," he would write in a letter from the Hotel Silmande in 1985. *"Many are just doing a job that pays ok but many are quite wonderfully inspired with the desire to help others. I'm not concerned with the managers who stay mostly in Ouaga, I mean the men and women who bring their families to stay 4–5 years or more and work on a single project to aid a village, a school or hospital or whatever. Progress is so painfully slow it is a wonder there isn't more cynicism. But then managing to ease the lives of even a few or few dozen people on one scale certainly should be more rewarding than, say, writing scrapbooks full of newspaper arti-*

cles." He was about to set off on a long trip through danger-ous country with a driver he couldn't understand in a car about which everyone had doubts on a road that turned to glue when it rained. "*Should be worth a paragraph or two.*"

As the conversations continued, I began to feel an unfa-miliar camaraderie with this diffident, mysterious man, as if under all the differences we were somehow kindred. An inti-macy developed, and something else besides. I was intensely attracted to him, and I began to see, in the way he let himself look at me, that the attraction was returned.

We didn't flirt—not in the way I defined it, anyway, hid-ing behind double entendres and practiced gestures, skip-ping between provocation and retreat, hoping to be followed but never found. Flirtation was the best of games, and I had always loved to play it with proper men like him, rubbing against their rectitude the way a yearling rubs the downy fuzz from his antlers against the bark of a tree. But this was foreign country to me. I felt no urge to conquer, no com-bustible alloy of anger and desire, no lie at the heart of it, none of the hollow druglike urgency that desire induced.

Instead we talked, and drank, and drank some more until it grew late and, looking deep into each other's eyes, we called for the check. Back on the street we smiled and said good night and got into separate cabs. What did he want? What did I?

It was not a question I had ever needed to ask myself. De-sire in its own right had always been enough. Until then I was entranced by the mere possibility of passion, the way it created its own reality, set in motion by the beauty of a man's forearm when he rolled up his sleeves or the way he raked his fingers through his hair. For such gestures, Virginia Woolf wrote, one falls in love for a lifetime. Or at least for a night. I loved the way the heart just turned and suddenly there was someone you wanted more than anything—or just as suddenly wanted no longer. I couldn't understand why anyone ever got married. Passion was perfect because it was unconnected to the real world, because it overwhelmed, at least for the moment, everything you were meant to be or were supposed to do, conferring the exuberant license of a snow day. In some obscure way I knew it was an escape of sorts, a balm for anxiety and a way to delay the future, but that had never seemed like much of a drawback.

Now Lescaze had come along and screwed the whole thing up. I had tried to turn him into a character in my latest fantasy, but he refused to play the part. He didn't have the kind of vanity that puffs up in the presence of admiration. I had tried to turn myself into a character he would find fascinating, but that hadn't worked either. He seemed to look right through my attempts with a kind of amused patience, as if waiting for me to simply settle down and be myself. As if he had seen the good in me and was just waiting for me to see it too.

That was the difference between him and all the others, I realized finally. He offered me the chance to connect the dots between my public and private selves, maybe even to find bedrock. And heart in throat, I took it.

"You're nervous," I said.

"No. Well, maybe. A little. How can you tell?"

"Because of the way you're stroking your tie."

He smiled. "I never knew I did that."

It was a warm windy night in early spring, disturbing, unsettling, premature. We were having drinks in the bar at the Hay-Adams Hotel, whose dim lighting and luxury suggested intrigue and secrecy. Recognized here, our presence would be more difficult to explain.

"What are we doing?" he asked abruptly.

"I don't know," I began. But I did know, had known all along, although until that moment I'd kept it a secret from myself. My stomach jumped, and I was aghast at the words I found myself saying, yet thrilled as well, as if diving off a cliff. "All I know is that I want to kiss you more than anything else in the world."

And then he leaned over the small table, pressing his tie to his chest with one hand, pulling my head toward his with the other, and I knew that there had never been a kiss like that in the whole of history.

A little while later he walked me to the parking garage across the street from the *Post*. "There's one thing you should know right now," he said. "Eventually we will be discovered. Sooner or later everyone will know."

He looked not frightened but determined, his intensity palpable. His words scared me and exalted me, the danger of it, the risk he was willing to run. Would it have been any different if I had known what would happen? No. Yes. No.

We met the next time at my apartment. I lived then in a tiny one-bedroom in the corner of an old stone building in Adams Morgan, a still affordable, shabby, and polyglot neighborhood, as yet ungentrified.

The living room was too small for the furniture it contained, a gold-and-blue-velvet-striped sofa of bargelike proportions and a nubbly tweed easy chair my mother helped me pick up at a discount furniture warehouse. The furniture was ugly, old-fashioned and comforting, like a bathrobe you wear when no one's around. And in fact I almost never invited people over. Now I wondered what it would look like to a man of such sophistication.

Lee arrived shortly after I did, and I was still out of breath from a last-ditch attempt to straighten up. He stopped short in the center of the room and seemed to hesitate for a moment; perhaps he was reconsidering his options. I looked with his eyes at the albums strewn over the floor, the cheap bookcases, the untempered fluorescent glare that emanated from the kitchen. He held his immaculate overcoat tentatively while looking for a place to put it. I took it from him and laid it apologetically on the easy chair. "There's no coat closet," I observed, as if noting its absence for the first time.

Music, I thought desperately, we need music. I sat down

on the floor looking for something to play, and Lee joined me, bemused. The sudden proximity made me dizzy. For the first time, nothing separated us, but I could not imagine making the first move. "I'm not sure I remember the last time I sat on the floor to do something," he said. "Do you spend much time down here?"

Not too much, I said, wondering what extensive floor sitting said about my character. Finally I found what I was looking for—Schubert's Quintet in C Major. Lee had told me over drinks one night that Rudolf Serkin considered the second movement music to enter heaven by. I put the music on and he smiled, touched that I had remembered.

Lee moved to the enormous sofa. I poured Jack Daniel's and sat down on the other end, about a hundred miles away, as if my parents were in the room next door. The kiss we had shared at the Hay-Adams sat between us, arms folded, tapping its foot, waiting for something to happen. Nothing did.

We talked, about Graham Greene, I think, too stupid with desire to make any sense, too afraid to do anything else. Lee stayed about two hours. And then, looking dazed and bewildered and utterly undone, he stood up, folded his overcoat neatly on his arm, and left.

It was the same the next time he came over, except that we drank martinis instead of whiskey and talked about Samuel Beckett instead of Greene. Which did I like better, the plays or the prose? I hadn't read the prose.

What was going on? Not just with him, with me. There

are moments in any erotic dance when the wind shifts or dies altogether, and the tension between the two of you simply disappears. But that was not what had hapened. I was poleaxed with desire and certain he was as well. Perhaps it was the enormity of the thing we contemplated that made our state of paralyzed indecision, no matter how exquisite, the safest place to stay.

When he left the third time (Wild Turkey, Ezra Pound) I decided things were better this way. So far we had done nothing wrong, and it was probably best to leave things as they were. Besides, sex would probably be an incredible disappointment after such a buildup. I couldn't reconcile such a romance as ours with the take-no-prisoners anarchy of eros. Lee was so decorous, so reserved, so perfectly elegant— I feared those qualities would follow him into the bedroom. And then one night I learned that I was more wrong than I had ever been.

Chapter Four

SOMETIMES I WONDER if the story would have been different had it not been spring. Washington was ravishing that April, and the fact that such extravagant loveliness flourished in a city so dedicated to compromise and prudence made almost anything seem possible. Even, perhaps, a love affair like ours.

I had never known anything like this, the simple gratitude at someone else's very existence, the dumb wonder of it. The real world dimmed, its sounds—typewriters, construction work, the neighbor's rock and roll—muffled by my constant state of reverie. For a time, even the dread inspired by writing paled now that I lived so brilliantly in the eyes of another.

In the newsroom a necessary decorum separated us, and that was part of the pleasure. We passed our secret back and forth in smiles, and sent each other stories through the computer, tales about girls with big feet and odd fellows who despaired over the New York Mets. We were delighted with ourselves, the way any two people are in that first psyche-delic transport of love. We were insufferable.

We met at odd hours, whenever we could, tethered to makeshift and camouflage. Early in the morning, he arrived racket in hand, because he was meant to be at a tennis game. Late at night, he was dressed in black tie, if an official White House dinner provided some elasticity in the time he was ex-pected home.

I felt a little as if I were in a play, where each scene is fi-nite, the actors look their best, the light is flattering, and the end is inevitable.

Our time together in the apartment became more real than anything else, the world reduced to a universe of two. Leaving it to find out otherwise was always a shock. One morning, I ran out to hail a cab in the driving rain, leaving Lee to shelter under the eaves, trying to save his twenty-year-old raw silk suit, made for him in Hong Kong and treasured through the years. A car slowed down—it was a fellow re-porter on his way to work, offering a ride. We drove off and I looked out the rear window to see Lee standing on the cor-ner, drenched and raising his hands in a comic gesture of surrender. It was disorienting, as if two separate realities had tried to occupy one space.

Sometimes I thought about what it would be like to browse through a book store with Lee or refer to him off-handedly in conversation with my friends. I had always treasured those moments in a love affair after the first time you make love, when you do together the small daily things you had previously done alone—*you like to wash? Great, I like to dry*—but stolen hours leave no room for the little routines of life. I did cook him dinner once, expanding my all-milk-shake repertoire in his honor to include, appropriately enough, a bluefish soaked in gin. But usually we burned the hours in bed, the only time we could be sure of each other, free from any other claims.

It was better this way, I thought. Lee would never see me in my second-best underwear, I would never see the hole in his sock. Our love affair would always be perfect. I was Lee's mistress: It was an old-fashioned but still sophisticated-sounding role, that put me in mind of Hepburn and Tracy, Callas and Onassis.

One night, I came home straight from the airport, having been out of town for a few days reporting a story. It was about eight o'clock in the evening. I had been travelling all day and hadn't talked to anyone, not even Lee, and I felt pleas-antly disengaged from the world, like a guest just strolling into a lively cocktail party. I put down the suitcase, poured a drink, and walked over to the living room window.

I had always loved being alone in my apartment at this time of night, when the dusky shadows closed in and the lamplight glowed low and golden. I liked to look out over the rooftops of the row houses and apartment buildings, safe in my own cave imagining all the lives lived behind other people's blinds and curtains: women chopping onions or yelling at their kids, fathers coming home, babysitters headed to homes of their own.

Lee's house was only one block over from my apartment. I could see the upper story windows from where I stood. The house was dark at first, but just as I turned to go, a light switched on behind the drawn curtains. Then a familiar silhouette appeared. He was putting on a shirt, the way I had seen him do many times at closer range, and then a tie, his head tilted back in that stiff awkward manner that men always seemed to adopt in front of a mirror. Must be going out, I thought. It felt strange not to know where he had been, where he was going. Had he noticed the lights in my apartment?

Then another silhouette appeared, a woman's silhouette. She walked toward him. The shadows blended into each other. I held my breath; were they about to kiss? No, she was just straightening his tie. I watched fascinated. I had no idea how to straighten a tie. With that simple act, his wife became real to me, as real as the women making dinner in the windows I liked so much to watch.

And yes, there were children in that house too.

I jerked back from the window as if I'd been slapped, wincing at my fantasies of what it meant to be a mistress. I was no headstrong prima donna whose genius somehow sanctioned her misadventures; I was the one wedged into the odd stolen moment, superfluous, like the extra adjective the night editor always cut from my copy. What did the Brits call it? A bit on the side.

In August the president repaired to the summer White House in Santa Barbara, and the White House press corps, Lee among them, followed. A few days after he left a telegram arrived. It read: "Absence diminishes an ordinary passion and increases great ones, as the wind extinguishes candles and fans the fire." I was impressed: he really was a good writer. The telegram was followed by a phone call. There wouldn't be much news to cover in Santa Barbara, which meant a lot of free time. Could I join him for a few days? I told him how much I liked his telegram. I'm glad, he said. The epigram, as he was sure I knew, was written by La Rochefoucauld.

Lee said he had found a small, charming, inexpensive inn tucked away in a quiet section of town. I pictured paradise, a rose-covered bungalow and a small terrace where the waiter would serve us our breakfast in a shower of dappled sunlight. What I found, after several days, two missed connections, and an epic exploration of the California highway system, was a seedy, dimly lit low-lying place done up in frayed brown shingles. At the front desk, a short, stocky, beetle-browed frowning man with a thick Bulgarian accent scowled and said that no, he didn't have a reservation for me, but he'd fix me up for twice the room rate and cash up front.

He showed me to a room with sour-smelling carpeting and bedsheets that made you want to sleep with your shoes on.

The kind of room where fugitive embezzlers and knocked-up secretaries come to bad ends, in old movies.

Waiting for Lee, I sat there in the dark planning my escape. I would not unpack. I would get on the next plane back east. But then there was a knock on the door, and Lee walked in, his voice full and throaty. Angel, he said, and took me in his arms, and then it was all right, the mildewed walls, the frowning Cerberus at the register, the panicked sense of unmooring.

We spent the night together, the whole night, for the first time. We didn't sleep much, each of us shifting uneasily, waking up disoriented, then remembering where we were. Through the long dark hours I lay awake, made uncomfortable by this presence next to me, the fact of him—something was bearing down fast, and I wanted to jump out of the way. But then it was morning and, drowsing in the reassuring sunlight, I let myself decide that the rest was just nightmare. Lee went to the daily briefing, and I headed for the beach.

I took a run, aiming for Lee's easy athleticism, but the role of healthy, disciplined person was still new to me, so I stopped and looked around instead. I had never been on a West Coast beach before. I wanted to feel condescending toward the whole scene, like a proper East Coast serious person, but in fact I liked it—the perfect bodies bobbing or gliding or rolling past, the air delicious, sweet, and clean, the innumerable shades of blond catching the light in a hundred different ways. Everyone was nearly naked and yet the effect was curiously asexual. They radiated an almost childish kind of happiness, the kind you can bite into, the kind that won't bite back.

Afterward I went to the hotel where the press corps was bivouacked, nervous as I walked through the plush, empty corridors that I would run into someone from Washington. When I got to Lee's room, the door was already open — he was on the telephone and held his hand up in warning, like a school crossing guard stopping traffic. "It's nothing, just the maid," he said into the phone. Of course he was talking to his wife. I wanted to send the vase of fresh jacarandas crashing loudly to the ground. When the call was over, he apologized. I said nothing.

The next day we drove to Big Sur. It was foggy; the coastline was revealed in intermittent flashes. Lee tuned the radio to an oldies station. Neither of us said much. At first the silence worried me: he will be bored, he will see how ordinary I am. But gradually I began to like this about us, the reticence, the things unsaid, the richness of the silence. Looking back, I would see that it was a sea change, that moment in a relationship when you let yourself breathe normally again, the moment when you are safe enough to be yourself and know that it is the same for him.

Proust wrote that from the moment they meet, lovers are in mourning for the end of their affair. The rest of the day slipped by dreamlike; I closed my eyes, wanting to lock in every bit of the happiness I felt, so that it would always be there for me to summon. And yet only now does it seem permissible to remember what that happiness was like, the airy benign nature of it. The memory surprised me, like the lost seashell or cat's-eye marble you find in a pocket years after small hands had given it into your safekeeping.

Our last day we drove to Venice Beach and walked down the boardwalk, among the strolling musicians and the gaunt junkies and the swirling crowds of tourists. There was a menace in the air, as if beneath the noise and the shouting street vendors and the drifting grifters and pickpockets, the street was braced for a bad moon rising.

Just then a naked woman crawled out of a doorway, on her belly, pulling herself onto the boardwalk. She was skinny, nearly emaciated, and the nipples on her small breasts were dark, like bruises. She was filthy; her fingernails curved into yellowed claws. Ragged brown hair covered her face. She was no older than I was. She muttered something in a cracked voice, but it was impossible to tell what hunger drove her, what nightmare she was trying to escape.

She made little progress before strong arms reached out of the same dark doorway and grabbed her feet. I watched, mesmerized, until I felt Lee's hand in the small of my back gently urging me away. He looked at me questioningly, as if to ask what I found so fascinating.

I have a friend who never passes a homeless woman on the street without giving her money. My friend is rich, beautiful, and successful, a woman who has emerged by her own resilience from more than her fair share of disasters. I asked her once why she did this: giving sometimes to the men but always to the women. Because one day, she said, it could be me.

"Women get a raw deal even when they get a good deal," a man I once knew liked to say.

I don't think my daughter will see the world this way. I doubt she will undermine her own accomplishments with the apprehension that she is in some way a fraud or that she is not entitled to the risks she takes. But every woman I knew worried, as I did, that the patch of ice they occupied was thin and could break at any moment, as it had for the woman on the boardwalk in Venice Beach.

I said none of this to Lee. I thought he was too well-assured of his place in the world to understand the simultaneous allure and fear with which I greeted risk. He proved me wrong, of course.

On our way to dinner our last night in Santa Barbara, Lee took my hand. He walked, as he always did, on the outside, closest to the street. But then he stopped and looked at me, his head slightly tilted to one side, his eyes for the moment unreadable. I was wearing a red silk dress, with thin straps, a tight bodice, and a flared skirt. I knew he liked vibrant colors. Was it the wrong thing to wear, at this hour, in this world, to this sort of place?

"What are you thinking?" I asked him.

"I was thinking that now I'm the man other men look at,"

he said. "The one I never thought I'd be, the one walking down the street with the beautiful girl." It had not occurred to me that just as he was my dream, I was his.

We drank champagne and toyed with the food. "What is to become of us?" he said, and my eyes filled with tears. It was a conversation that could go nowhere, because there was nowhere for it to go.

I thought somehow it would continue that way forever, secret and privileged. Love affairs were separate from daily life, like Church and State. They took place out of time, disconnected from reality. At least ours did for most of a year, until the day Shelby Coffey was promoted to deputy managing editor and Bradlee named his successor: Lee Lescaze.

We tried to stop seeing each other and, for a while, we did. We spoke only about story ideas. We met only within the glass walls of his office. We avoided eye contact. I don't remember who cracked first. It didn't matter. He had become necessary, that's all. Like air or water or ground beneath my feet.

We tried to be discreet, but proximity destroyed our attempts at deception. I found out later that people had figured it out long before we thought they did: it was, after all, a newsroom. Our conversations on the phone were duly noted: it was easy to see through the glass walls that we hung up at the same time. Friends started asking me questions. I denied everything but not all that convincingly—on some level, I wanted people to know. I hadn't realized how tired I was of being a secret.

For weeks the tension hummed around us and we lived in the murk of what everyone knew and no one acknowledged, the rumors circling like flies. We didn't talk about it much. We were curiously passive, like sleepwalkers. I think we both needed to get to the brink of something, whatever it was, however it ended. And so we looked away, as the glass separating us from the world grew more transparent and more brittle.

Until it broke.

In April I sent him a gift, to mark the anniversary of the night we became lovers. I spent a long time at the florist shop near Dupont Circle, discussing a flower arrangement that wouldn't look too frou-frou to send to a man. We settled finally on a single orchid surrounded by moss and a piece of wood, I think—it looked spare and Japanese. I wrote out a card to be sent with it. "Thank you," it read, "for the most wonderful year of my life." And signed my name.

He must have put the card in his wallet, along with the credit card receipts and a note to himself to pick up the dry-cleaning, the sort of stuff a man empties out of his pockets at night and leaves in a drawer or on top of a dresser in the bedroom, because that's where his wife finally found it.

Chapter Five

IT WAS A CLOSE, muggy morning in May. I was at home, working on a story. When Lee's call came, I had been in the kitchen indulging in the small procrastination of making tea. "Brace yourself," he said. His wife knew about us. Soon so would everyone else.

I hung up the phone and stared hard out the kitchen window, as if the solidity of things made of concrete and brick would convince me the news wasn't real. I looked toward the National Cathedral, hoping for comfort I suppose, but all I could see was the towering construction crane that loomed over it, sliced across the sky like a jagged scar. I walked into the bedroom, lay down on the wrinkled sheets, pulled the covers high over my head, and fell instantly asleep.

I was afraid to go into the newsroom and so at lunch Lee came to me. He looked tired but unnervingly calm, braced for battle. He was almost relieved, he said, that the news was out.

We talked about what would happen next. His wife

wanted them to go into counseling together. He didn't see the point. Lee didn't believe in therapy—he had come of age in the fifties, when analysis was the trendy thing to do in sophisticated New York circles. To him, it was a narcissistic fad attractive to the weak-minded.

"I think you should try," I said. The sound of my voice startled me. Lee was angry. "Why? You sound as if you don't want me to leave her."

What I should have said was this: *I don't know what I want. I never meant for this to happen. I am a thirty-year-old girl with the moral depth of a dragonfly, and you would be crazy to do anything that connected your happiness to mine. I'm not ready. I'll never be ready. Work it out with your wife.*

Instead I said, "I just mean that you owe it to her to try. So that when you leave, she'll know you gave it every chance."

The next morning I walked through the newsroom, past the row upon row of desks in a nimbus of shock and embarrassment and a sickening fear. Judgment hung in the air, embodied by a whisper that stopped when I passed by, a glance hastily averted, a barely concealed disdain. Or so it seemed to me. Memory is smoke from the stories we once told ourselves.

Everyone loves a scandal; it's the train wreck that didn't happen to you. In the past I had been a participant in the gleeful gossip that always surrounded hidden folly come to light. Now the condescending spiteful buzzing hummed in my head.

I lived on crazy time, emergency room time. I veered with equal certainty from hope to despair. I would walk to work in the morning feeling certain that I was in love and worried only that I would lose Lee. But then, in the newsroom, I would catch sight of Bradlee's cold, unsmiling face, or the vein in Shelby's temple throbbing double-time, and then I would lurch back to the career I was screwing up, the disapproval I was reaping, and the mad math would begin again, trying to come up with a solution that would make everyone happy. Or, for that matter, anyone.

I looked for advice. I had many friends who told me what I wanted to hear, but only one who told me what I needed to know.

Julia had been a reporter on the Virginia desk when I met her my first year at the paper. Now she was on leave to write a book. She came from Detroit, where she had been an activist in the antiwar movement and worked in one of the city's first rape crisis centers. She had a passionate adventurous spirit—she had quit graduate school to cover the antiapartheid struggle in South Africa, undeterred by the lack of money or the lack of assignment. Always she saw the world that lay beyond the limits of her personal drama, a perspective with which I had no experience. And yet we found common ground—she too had her night stories and her secrets.

She met me in the gravel yard of her weekend house. She was beautiful but never acted as if she noticed; her features were fine and delicately sketched, a small upturned

nose, perfectly honed cheekbones, a cat's opacity to her al-
mond eyes.

Julia dragged me about the garden and the barnyard first,
before letting me into the house, pointing out each budding
basil leaf, every cloven foot, bringing me up to date on the
state of the rosebush and what solid foods the baby was now
eating.

"What do you think?" she asked at the end of the tour.

"I'm wondering if there will ever be a point in our friendship where you don't force me to look at every blade of grass
in the backyard while listening to your latest plan for rear-
ranging the living room."

"Absolutely not," she said, and she was right: it would be
the same in the big house on Sutton Place and within the elegant confines of Sloane Square and later in the airy little
apartment where she lived after the divorce.

We went into the house then, and I played with the baby
while she sautéed some chicken. I wasn't hungry, but she
made me eat it, and the fact that I was still worth nourishing
made me a little less wretched.

Afterward we sat in her living room. Lace curtains filtered
the light cast on silent curves of old African pottery, everyday
bowls and teacups made poignant by all that had shattered in
the long centuries they had somehow survived. Julia's long,
thin, delicate fingers patted the coffee table, as if she were
patting down the wild disorder of my life.

"So. How are you?"

I tried to be clever in lieu of being honest. "I think about Pompeii a lot."

Explain, please.

"You know what it's like when you first see Pompeii? It feels like it happened just yesterday. When I was there, I imagined this bright sunny day and a woman like me walking down the street to the market like she does every morning. She's thinking about all the dumb stuff we all think about, like can she afford a new toga or the good-looking man at last night's banquet, when somebody screams. She looks up and she can't believe it: a river of fire is headed her way. The last thing she thinks is 'Oh fuck, I've wasted my life!' I feel like that."

I waited for her to smile, but instead she cast me a look that told me that this latest misadventure of mine did not provoke the amused tolerance of the others.

Julia now saw it all from the other shore. She was the first of my friends to get married, the first to have a child.

"I know what you're going to say," I said. "But I really love him."

"What you feel isn't the important thing," she said. The idea startled me, and I looked up. Hadn't that always been enough? "There's a wife," she said. "There are children. You can't know what it means to tear something like that up. It's wrong. You have to walk away."

"I don't think I can," I said.

·   ·   ·

Lee's therapy didn't last long. Within a few weeks the doctor said it was clear that he had no interest in saving his marriage.

Becky, his wife, continued to see the psychiatrist. Understandably, she passed along to Lee any insight into the situation that might undermine his resolve, and he brought them all to me, hoping I would make them disappear.

"Becky's therapist says you're predatory," Lee said.

"You say it like it's a bad thing." I tried to smile, but it felt like I had a face full of novocaine.

He tried too, with similar success. His eyes were troubled. He hesitated.

"He also says you'll betray me with someone else. That women like you always leave."

Women like me. The words scalded, summoning up old clichés: the scarlet woman in the tacky satin dress, the feather boa, and the fuck-me shoes, burning down the life of a good man led astray. If only, I thought. I could have used the heartlessness that traditionally went along with the package.

The caricature stung. But was the fantasy in which I had wrapped myself any less ridiculous? It had been "so pleasant," as Anthony Trollope wrote, "to feel oneself to be naughty! There is a Bohemian flavor of picnic about it which, though it does not come up to the rich gusto of real wickedness, makes one fancy that one is on the border of that delightful region in which there is none of the constraint of custom—where men and women say what they like, and do what they like."

In the sixties, bad behavior had been almost a sacrament, a declaration of independence from the old repression and conformity. Transgression had seemed so glamorous, a way out of the ordinary. Over the years, as I cast about for heroes, I had constructed something of a shrine to famously wayward women, for whom passion was an inextricable part of the bargain they struck with fortune, who measured their progress by the lines they crossed. They were an odd lot, culled from legend and literature—Salome, Madame de Maintenon, Zelda Fitzgerald, George Sand, Billie Holiday, Marlene Dietrich, Janis Joplin. Among them were sirens and divas, failures and fuckups, courtesans and geniuses, the ones who got away with it and also the ones who didn't.

For a long time, I had needed these women, all of them. They weren't martyrs to me, they were fighters with the scars to prove it, who had found a kind of glory in the most hazardous and alarming part of their uncompliant hearts. But I never looked at the pain they caused or how valuable was the wreckage they left in their wake.

Now I had crashed into the matrix of cause and effect, of responsibility and guilt, into the world of adults. I didn't know what to do. I didn't know who to be. I felt too guilty then, and too ashamed, to see that moment for what it was: the beginning of my growing up.

Messengers from the front returned with daily dispatches. I heard them all. What the editors thought, what their spouses said, how Lee drank, how Becky cried. What was left of the cynic in me was amazed at the number of instant converts to the sacredness of the marriage vow that my conduct had apparently created.

None of my personal shortcomings, however irrelevant, went unexamined. One night the phone rang minutes after I'd finally fallen asleep.

"I just saw Becky," said a friend just back from an embassy reception. "She was saying that even though everyone thinks you're so thin, you have a really fat ass."

"Jesus. Do I?"

"No. Not really. Well, maybe in your red skirt."

At the center of attention you are curiously alone. I went to see a therapist. By then anxiety was making it hard to breathe, my left arm was numb, and I couldn't open my mouth more than a couple of inches—temporary mandible paralysis, said the doctor. Something to do with stress.

The therapist was a tall, thin woman with short faded red hair and a smile I somehow trusted. She told me to call her Jean—she didn't like formal titles. Jean gave me a paper bag to breathe into; it helped a little. She asked me about Lee.

"Some of my friends say I'm looking for a father figure," I told her.

"No kidding," she said drily. "What do you intend to do?"

"I don't know," I said. "I feel like the train has left the station without me."

"What you have to work on is who's in charge here," she said. "Who is making the decisions about what is happening to you? Because it's not Lee or your parents or even the magic you think writes your stories for you. Until you see yourself as the creator of your own life, your anxiety will remain."

"In that case," I said, "I'm going to need a lot more paper bags."

Once the news reached the *Post* hierarchy, things happened quickly. None of my old career worries mattered now. I was just a problem to be solved. I couldn't stay in Style, and as a features writer, the options were somewhat limited. I was transferred to the Sunday magazine, then a kind of editorial Siberia, unread, unmentioned, uninteresting. Could have been worse, someone said in an attempt at comfort. Could have been obits.

By the middle of July two months after her discovery of the note, Lee and Becky decided that he would move out of the house at the end of the month.

The night before Lee arrived, I sat alone in my apartment drinking Jack Daniel's and listening to *La Traviata*, which seemed fitting under the circumstances. I was frightened by the future, but I was also angry with myself. I thought about what Jean, the therapist, had said. And it seemed to me that I had become a story without an author. My life had been shaped always by others—first by my parents and then by my lover and then by the authorities to which we both answered, and when it most mattered, I had taken no active hand in what was to become of me. At that moment I felt as if, in this crucial event in my life, I had failed my test, my rite of passage.

But I was wrong. I *had* chosen, although I only understood that many years later. The past can surprise you, yielding gifts from nearly forgotten ground.

I didn't know it then, but I had chosen Lee that day in the kitchen, following his wife's discovery of the note I had written him. It had happened when he told me he wanted to leave his marriage. At first I had tried to buy time by advising him to wait. He thought I was trying to tell him that I didn't want him after all.

I have always remembered the anger in his voice and the panic in mine. What I had forgotten was this: how something had made me turn to look at him then, and when I did, when I saw what was written on his face, his hope and love and trust, his courage and his surprise at the turn his life had taken, his fear that he might be out there all alone, with no one at his side, I knew absolutely what I wanted. I wanted never to leave him. It was an instant, obscured immediately by all that followed, buried for years under the compost of guilt and consequence. But now the memory is mine again, adamant and eternal.

I had chosen after all, the matter settled by the look on a face, the leap of a heart. To know that lightens everything.

·　·　·

On a hot muggy Sunday morning at the end of July, Lee walked out the door of his three-story town house and around the corner and into my two-room apartment. He brought an old maroon canvas and leather monogrammed suitcase and his tennis racket.

We stared at each other across the narrow living room. Our life together lay before us, a sleeping dog we had to find a home for.

Finally I said, "Are you sure?"

"Yes," he said. "Are you?" I nodded and tried not to let him see how frightened I was that he had invested his future in such shaky funds.

The next morning I watched him walk around my apartment in just his jeans. He looked older, more vulnerable, the flesh a little loose on his chest and around his waist. Which of my flaws would he notice, now that he had the time to find them? We moved around each other cautiously for the next few days, breathing a strange, thin air. There was so much I didn't know. I didn't know what he liked to eat for breakfast or whether he liked his socks rolled or folded. I didn't know if it was my job to know these things. I thought about the Jack Daniel's in the cupboard and the ice cream in the freezer. I thought of the coleus plant in my living room window, curled and mottled with brown, the small heap of dead leaves on the floor. How will I keep him alive? I wondered. As if he were an orchid whose care had been entrusted to me. I hadn't even thought to make him a key.

Early in the fall we moved to a larger apartment on the first floor of an old stone building. The windows fronted on Columbia Road, a broad and busy street, opening our lives to the inspection of anybody passing by or waiting at the bus stop. Still, it took us a while to buy wooden shutters for them: I think the exposure too accurately reflected the way we felt for us to even notice.

We had very little furniture, only the few pieces from my old apartment and the small black and white television my parents had given me when they moved on to color. Eventually, Lee brought over a few things from the attic of his old life: a couple of worn Indian and Pakistani rugs, a wooden bookcase with beveled glass doors, and a dining room table and chairs his father had designed for their town house in New York. The chairs were a cold and uncomfortable geometry of chrome, corduroy, and right angles, but the table was beautiful, a long rectangular piece of polished pearwood; underneath there was a buzzer for summoning the butler.

To this we added our first mutual purchases: a fifties-style nightstand, a hulking pair of deeply scratched matching dressers, a dozen oyster forks and a black futon, against the day his children would come to stay with us. Whenever we spoke, a slight echo answered from the bare walls.

Now a man's suits hung in the closet, and I was suspended between the old life and the new, between solitude and the complicated process of living with a man. I liked it,

I resented it, and I wondered what Lee must think of this sudden shabbiness, this fall from grace.

I had longed for an end to all of the drama, to the return of an ordinary dailiness, but once it began, I remembered that I'd never been much good at that sort of life. Banished from Style, I hated work. Now I was the object of concern and amusement. One of my old colleagues gave me a sympathetic smile when I passed her desk. Then I heard her whisper to the reporter at the next desk, "Great career move, don't you think?" I can still hear the laughter.

I couldn't think of a thing to write, and no one had an assignment for me, and so during the day I would wander the streets of downtown Washington, a bad place to be adrift, filled as it is with the relentlessly purposeful and productive. Could it be that I envied them? A fine rebel I had turned out to be.

I sold my sexy black turbo-charged Mustang in the fall. I had loved that car; now it was an embarrassing reminder of a cast-off fantasy. Besides, we needed the money. Lee's salary went to his wife and children; we lived on my considerably smaller wages and the money Lee won in a weekly high-stakes poker game.

One Saturday afternoon, running errands in the neighborhood, we passed a pet store. A bored gray parrot stared out the window from a wooden perch. I would have passed on, but Lee was curious: he had always loved birds. We went in just to look.

A few hours later we emerged with a young cockatiel, gray and white with a tuft of yellow feathers on his head and a patch of orange on his cheeks that made him look like an indignant clown. We named him Elver. We liked the way it sounded, however oddly it applied to a bird—an elver is a baby eel. Maybe that's why we liked it, because it did apply so oddly and yet so perfectly to him, and also to us; we were all of us fish out of water.

Elver became the lightning rod for our disorder. We left his wings unclipped, and he spent his days, while we were at work, flying wildly around the apartment and roosting on the pots and pans. In the mornings he would sit on the curtain rod in the shower screaming the one phrase that sounded remotely like English. "Bend your ear!" he squawked. "Bend your ear bend your ear bend your ear!" In the evenings he would patrol the coffee table on foot, making endless circumnavigations, biting any unwary toe he happened to encounter. He made our lives impossible. We took a bleak solace in his bad behavior, even loved him for it.

In the evenings Lee tried to teach me how to play squash. I was hopeless—racket sports had been for rich people when I was growing up, and I had no hand-eye coordination that either of us could detect. Still, I liked it: it was wonderful to walk into an empty white room, to spend an hour unable to worry, to do anything but think of the current location of a small hard ball.

Lee gave up after a while—he loved squash too much to play it badly. We went back to a mutual pleasure. We had no proper glasses, and so he made the martinis in jelly jars, filled to the brim, great washtubs of oblivion. We would have two or three of those. We were reading *Under the Volcano*, and so we christened this time of day the Geoffrey R. Firmin Memorial Cocktail Hour, in honor of Lowry's mad alcoholic visionary fuckup. Jeff Time, for short.

Martini highs are very different from the ones that come from whiskey or rum. Whiskey warms, rum quickens. Martinis are cold in their kindness; they take away the doubts and offer instead the sadly inevitable.

We drank because we couldn't talk. There was so much not to talk about. Every night the first edition of the next day's paper was sent to all the section heads to catch any last-minute mistakes and iron out any space problems. Lee would look at Style and call the desk, and I would implode with jealousy and pain. I missed my old job, and I was furious that I had had to leave. But I couldn't tell Lee that; it would sound too much like regret.

Lee, for his part, was choking on the guilt he felt at leaving his children, but he insisted everything was fine. One night he went back to his old house after Becky called to say that Adrien, his three-year-old, would not go to sleep unless his father sang his favorite song to him. I knew the lyrics; I couldn't imagine how he got through them. *You are my sunshine, my only sunshine, you make me happy when skies are gray, you'll never know, dear, how much I love you, please don't take my sunshine away.*

I wanted to comfort him, but he couldn't talk about it. There were no words.

We couldn't talk about anything. Instead we fought. Badly at first, because neither of us knew how. We could not speak about all the damage we had done, all the guilt he was feeling, all the shock I was reeling from, because to speak about them would be to acknowledge the possibility that we had in fact smashed things up badly. So we fought about the inconsequential things that were the clues to all that we didn't know about each other and would have to learn.

Once, while I was cleaning the tub, I splashed him with water in a moment of playfulness that was only a thin veil for the fury I felt. He left the room in outrage, and I didn't know if he was coming back.

On another afternoon we prepared to have lunch with one of his closest friends, whom I was meeting for the first time. Lee dared to suggest that I was wearing too much makeup. He was right: it was too much makeup. I had tried too hard to look more grown-up. But no one had ever felt free to criticize my appearance, to make that sort of claim. I walked out and I wasn't sure if I was coming back.

Work made Lee tense, withdrawn. He was grumpy and hard to like. The time he spent with his children, whom I was not yet allowed to meet, was usually a disaster. He would come back angry and unwilling to admit it, which in turn angered me: I was sick of trying to guess his moods. "Great," he muttered, as he disappeared into the Sports section of the paper. "My children, my mistress, my boss, they all hate me."

One night Lee went out to a black-tie dinner, the fortieth birthday party of one of his closest friends at the paper. He came home very late and very drunk, so drunk he could barely walk, or talk for that matter. He needed to be undressed and put to bed, but I didn't understand that. Instead, I watched him coldly as he stood swaying in the doorway, a look of dopey curiosity on his face. His eyebrows arched the way they did when he was about to say something light and witty, but something short-circuited, and suddenly he fell, rather gracefully under the circumstances, flat on his face, his tuxedo starkly elegant against the scuffed planked wood of the floor.

The next day he slept late, and I left the house early, determined to find fresh sorrel leaves. I had recently bought a cookbook, my first, and in it I had come across a beautiful photograph of cream of sorrel soup, green and elegant in a gilt-edged cream-colored bowl. I had never even heard of sorrel. I can't explain it now—I couldn't explain it then— but I had this idea that if I could just make the perfect bowl of cream of sorrel soup, then I would be the kind of person who could fit in to this new life, I would be competent and know the things it was important for adults to know.

When Lee finally woke up, red-eyed and unshaven, I was in the kitchen struggling with a pot lid, a large domed thing that had long ago lost the little knob on top, making its removal from a hot skillet an operation for the nimble and the brave. He left the house without a word, which was all right, since I wasn't speaking to him.

But as soon as he was gone, I missed him. I had wanted to be revolted, to find in this sorry sodden mess of a man the wick to my indignation and regret. Instead I saw something else. I saw how hard this year had been, not for me, but for him, how much it had cost him, how terrible the bonfire that was burning all around him. Then I wanted him back, to hold him and comfort him, to apologize for not understanding. But I didn't know where he had gone.

He came back about twenty minutes later, with a small brown paper bag. Inside was a wooden knob and a screw, and before long he had fixed it to the pot lid. I was charmed: in my world, broken things stayed broken, until you threw them away.

That's when I knew that neither one of us was leaving, that we would fight and the walls would stand. I knew this, not in the way that you know you love someone, but in the way you learn, for the first time, that you are finally in a place from which you will not walk away.

It's been over twenty years since that morning in the kitchen. Everything has changed and most of it is gone. But I still have that lid, and the wooden knob still holds.

Chapter Six

A HOT, WINDLESS day at the end of August. Gray waves slapped listlessly at the indifferent shore. It was the armpit of the afternoon, the hour when the engine dies, when the humming rhythm of the day suddenly falls silent. We stood there, my lover's children and I, on top of a small grassy dune. The water was full of jellyfish. The sandwiches were gritty. There was nothing to drink. There was no energy for sandcastles, no fund of shared jokes to draw on, not even a car in which to escape, because their father had the car, their father, who was free in the city while I was trapped on this Delaware beach deep in the throat of summer.

I looked over my shoulder to find the children staring at me, waiting. What were they waiting for? Then I understood: they were waiting for me. Whether they liked me or not, whether they had any faith in my judgment, at that moment I was all there was. I was the adult and therefore the one who decided what would happen next. The simplicity of it staggered me. Not just their assumption that I was in fact a grown-up, but the weight of it, the irrefutable evidence it offered of something I had always considered very much in play—my own place in the world, the question of whether I had one. I had no idea what to do.

Lee's children and I had known each other for nearly a year by then. I had met them the day Miranda, the middle child, turned ten. She and her sister and her brother had stood in the hallway of our apartment, close to the door, heads bowed, as their father congratulated his younger daughter on what he called her entrance into double digits. He meant to be amusing, but the attempt fizzled; that was not what they were looking for.

Lee introduced me. I had expected to see hatred in their faces, but instead I found something much worse. It was the look one saw in newspaper photos of people standing in the wreckage of their house after the hurricane moved through—the stunned wonder of the survivor.

I tried a little speech. "I'm really nervous, and I guess you probably are too," I said, with a bright mechanical smile. "I know this is very awkward and difficult right now, but I really hope that we can be friends and learn about each other and that I can be of help to you in any way I can."

The children looked around vaguely, as if for a translator, or a rescue helicopter.

Alexandra, the eldest, was thirteen. Her beauty had just begun to emerge—long wavy blonde hair, large hazel eyes, her body a clash of braces and growing breasts. She was her mother's champion in the face of her father's perfidies. Behind the impassive mask of adolescence, her anger radiated; she shimmered with it.

She scared me a little. No: she scared me a lot. I was like a teenage boy sometimes, trying to impress her with how cool I was. At the beach I drove her around wearing a tank top and cut-off blue jeans, barefoot, steering with my right hand, my left arm dangling out the window. I drove the way the very first teenager I had ever known had driven, a girl whose soul I had wanted simply to possess. From her I had learned the essentials of driving. All the rest—steering, stopping, parking—was detail.

But Alexandra wasn't impressed. I wasn't old enough to be her mother, I wasn't young enough to be her friend, and when I tried to seek rapport by telling her about my own teenage insecurities around boys, she only looked sorry for me. She knew, and she was right, that she would never have that problem.

Sometimes we would form a temporary alliance, usually when she was fighting with her sister and needed to underscore her status as the eldest. Then we would consult about the menu, or whether Adrien should have a snack. Even then she was vigilant: we would share a moment we both found amusing and turn to each other smiling—until she remembered who I was and her face would cloud and she would turn away.

Miranda, dark-haired, dark-eyed, was more timid, yet occasionally there would be a fitful invitation in the way she looked at me. Eventually we began to find a common ground in make-believe. We invented characters, a rich heiress and a sleazy playboy, a snooty French waiter and a difficult customer, characters who could talk to each other more freely than we could, who could tease each other and laugh with each other in a way that she and I had not yet managed. Once when we were walking, she reached out and held my hand. But a few moments later her sister looked back, and Miranda jumped away as from a small electric shock.

Adrien, the youngest, was four years old, too young to keep up his own resistance for long. Still, our connection was intermittent. Sometimes he decided that whatever my faults, I was an endless source of silliness and entertainment, not quite as good as the TV but a suitable backup. But other times I was only the wall that kept him from his father.

And then there was me—the nonmother, the woman who took away their father, the nonfriend, the not-anything, the stranger superimposed on all that should be safe and familiar.

The first weekend the children had spent with us began on a gray and chilly Saturday in November, the kind I used to spend when I lived alone under the covers reading books of dubious merit and chatting on the phone with my friends.

Their father showed them the room that would be theirs whenever they came to visit—a white-walled, high-ceilinged square, with scuffed wood floors and bars on the street-level window. I still wince when I think what it looked like— empty, except for the black futon in a corner, an ironing board in the center of the floor, a few opened but unpacked moving boxes tumbled about, to which some ragged bits of masking tape still clung. But the children said nothing.

Then they waited and I waited for Lee to tell us what we were going to do, but Lee merely smiled and asked Adrien if he needed to go to the bathroom, and Alexandra and Miranda if they wanted a snack. Then he sat down in the one shabby easy chair, picked up the newspaper, and disappeared from view.

Lee was still reading the front section when the children and I finished our third game of Candy Land. The sports pages lasted through at least four hundred rounds of Go Fish. By the time he finished the foreign news, the girls were watching with glazed eyes as Adrien pretended to be a tiny chick just hatching from an empty box as I clucked encouragement on the side. By then I was in a hyperbolic state of silliness, chattering any nonsense that came to mind, a night-club comic playing to the recently bereaved, trying to patch over the bleak silence that lay just under the surface and to control my own fury at the way Lee had abandoned us.

I had to admire their sangfroid, then and in all the

strange, chilly months that followed, the way they watched our desultory attempts at housekeeping, my frantic efforts in the kitchen, the large drinks we poured to force ourselves through the tension that stopped our tongues. Lee's own Swiss father had been an austere, elegant man, distant and formal with his son. Lee was much the same back then, dumb with love, unable to speak. The children saw the way their father hid behind a newspaper when they came to visit; what they could not see was the guilt he was hiding from, his face crumpled with the pain he had caused them.

For months we lurched from weekend to weekend that way, a forced and intermittent family. By summer, after it had been a year since he left, Lee wanted to take the children away to neutral ground for a real vacation, and his wife reluctantly agreed.

And so we rented a house sight unseen in Rehoboth Beach, and Lee borrowed a friend's beat-up brown station wagon to get us there. When we drove up to the front door of Lee's old house to collect the children, their mother stepped out to say goodbye. I slunk down low in the front seat, straightening up only when we had backed out of the driveway and driven off to our holiday, our first as this strange conformation of people that had no history, no name, no sense of the future. The only thing we shared then was the dread we each brought with us.

And yet a part of me was grateful for this time away, for a

chance to exchange the bleakness of the newsroom for the windy simplicity of the beach, where panic was out of place and pleasure would assert itself, a place that was anywhere but the newsroom I used to love.

I was "drifting" at the *Post*—that was the way various editors put it—and drifting meant I was in trouble. The stories I wrote I wrote well enough, but there were not enough of them. Bradlee avoided eye contact, and Shelby was distant and vague. This upset me, but Elizabeth was not surprised. "You're a lost sheep now," she said. "You caused them problems, and no writer is worth that to them."

I lived in a state of skittery apprehension that prickled the skin and hobbled sleep and sent me wandering through the ghostly new apartment nearly every night. I would pace the rooms, gliding past Lee in the bed and the cockatiel asleep on the skillet hanging on the kitchen wall, shadowy forms in an unfamiliar world. I turned my head away when I passed the empty second bedroom, the one in which the children slept, the one in which they were careful to leave no trace. The smell of fresh paint still clung to the walls, and I would feel a little sick, my chest tight, my eyes wide open. I walked until I could breathe again or until I was too tired to walk anymore.

After a few months I fetched up on the city desk, as an assistant editor. I was there to help out with the daily deadline flood of copy that filled the inside of the Metro section—cops and robbers and traffic tie-ups and school board meetings — I was pretty sure the one in Arlington was the very same meeting in which I had once fallen asleep.

The idea was proposed as a temporary solution. But I knew what it really meant: career over. I would spend my life as a drone on the metro desk, laughed at by my former colleagues and despised as a piece of faded fluff by my new ones, the tough-minded reporters I had admired but had never wanted to be. Taking my seat at the maze of editors' desks for the first time, I felt lonely and out of place. It wasn't obits, I told myself. But it was close.

In the car on the way to the beach, the girls had been silent and Adrien, aware that every mile took him still farther away from his mother, was guarded, refusing to look at me or to sit on my lap. "We'll have fun," I had said to him. "I'll have fun with my dad," he answered.

The house we had rented turned out to be about two blocks from the beach in a tidy little community of prim vacation houses and scrupulously tended lawns. The neighborhood was a bit starchy, but the house itself was lovely — its three bedrooms and kitchen and living room all radiated around an atrium that was screened in at the top and complete with a picnic table and chaises longues and topiary and trailing coleus plants. The back yard was dense with pine trees and home to robins and red-winged blackbirds.

In the days that followed, we settled into a routine of sorts. I made breakfast in the morning, cereal when I was lazy, French toast when I wasn't, and then we walked in slow procession to the beach and drowned the hours in a trickle of drip castles and mad dashes into the waves, the cries of the children inextricable from the cries of the seagulls. In the late afternoon Lee played tennis with the girls, while Adrien scrambled after balls. At night we ate hamburgers and hot dogs and corn on the cob and steamed crab. In wet weather we played charades as the rain came misting in through the screening over the center of the atrium, and it felt as if we were living in the center of a large aviary.

The children as a group were full of energy and noise and constant demands, which kept Lee and me in constant motion. We smiled hello to each other in passing, as if we were acquaintances at a crowded party. Everyone was a little relieved; the five of us formed a group with a personality and an attitude of its own, and I began to breathe more easily.

But then the phone call from the *Post* had come, summoning Lee to a meeting in Washington. He would be gone for a couple of days.

Before he left, I took a long walk on the beach, wanting only to get away from this tangled mess of hurt, to be myself again. I walked for hours, alone in the way I'd been craving. At first the solitude felt torn and porous, but soon the silence settled in and I remembered why the shore had always been the place I had gone to escape.

My last extended beach trip had been nearly five years ago, at the end of my first year at the *Post*. Three weeks had stretched before me, empty of work, my first legitimate holiday from my first real job. The trip would always be the apogee of everything that is glorious about being young.

I had traveled with a friend of mine from the paper, a young woman nearly the same age as I was, our friendship fashioned from the mutual pursuit of good times and better clothes. We had rented a wonderful car, an enormous gray Oldsmobile with power everything and a plushy interior in a shade of red rarely seen outside a bordello.

Both of us were in recovery at the time, Carrie from a broken heart and I from the exhaustion of trying to be a competent human being. We drove down to a small barrier island at the end of the Outer Banks in North Carolina. We had chosen Ocracoke because it was as close to nowhere as we could get. Rich people hadn't found it yet and the island was still beautiful, comprising only a small fishing village that curved around a quiet harbor and, just beyond it, seven miles of federally protected Carolina coast.

Every morning was the same, walking down the empty highway dressed in a bikini—the only one in the whole store that had conferred even a slight illusion of bosom—cut-offs, and bug spray, then turning in past grassy dunes to the beach, where the waves stretched endlessly away, pluming in the high wind, parading, row upon ragged processional row, to the shore.

We took long walks and saw no one; we swam, we dozed,

we read, and watched with lazy interest the tossing of the sea reeds, green and red and brown, and the dainty incessant voracious hunt of the terns and the piping plovers and the black-winged skimmers.

We stayed all day and late into the afternoon. The wind buried our towels in the sand, changing them into mysterious runes, and the last of the light turned the cascading waves to melting silver, blurring the boundary between the shining water and the endless sand and the bleached sky, leaving nothing but the beauty of a barren moon.

Toward the end there was even a boy, lagniappe to an already perfect happiness. He was tall and long-limbed, with sandy blond hair and golden skin and strong graceful hands, and there was a delight to be had in simply looking at him. His mouth was wide and full lipped and parked in a crooked smile. His blue eyes were for rent, and his talk was slow, a California surfer's drawl made slurry from the long years of pot and Quaaludes. He was stupid, I realized sadly.

Then someone told me that he was not the shrimp-boat captain he professed to be, but a real-life smuggler, trading in bales of marijuana.

He was still stupid. But now he was perfect.

By the end of the three weeks, I was as self-contained and seamless as an egg, the scattered parts and shifting elements—writer and seductress and frightened girl—no longer strung out like paper lanterns along the way. I was ready for whatever came next. When you are young, you want to fly into the future; only time can teach you respect for the knives that are hidden there.

But all that happened in a different world. Now I walked alone under a gray sky, toward a house of unhappy children, slowing my steps the closer I got. I had promised to be back in an hour. Lee left for Washington as soon as I returned. The children and I watched him drive off. It was the first time we had ever been alone together.

The sudden sharp cry of a seagull brought me back to the stupefying, interminable afternoon. Alexandra and Miranda had wandered down the beach, but Adrien was still waiting.

Ever since Lee left, Adrien and I had had clamorous rows, because he was angry, because he was four, because his mother was not there. He would beg to go to the beach and, when we were finally ready, refuse to leave the house. Or he would go part of the way and then sit down, a small tornado of fury, in the gravel on the side of the road. Then I would pick him up, red-faced with anger myself, and carry him screaming in my arms, while his sisters walked stolidly ahead, pretending not to know us.

But Adrien was quiet now, uncertain, and withdrawn. His sisters had gone off to swim, but he shook his head when I asked if he wanted to join them. And so we walked along until we came to a small grassy dune that was covered in a trailing vine and patches of clover. I stopped, remembering this particular weed from one of the many places I had lived as a child. It was about a quarter-inch thick, with a flexible tensile strength and a density of narrow green leaves. I pulled out two of the vines, which clung stubbornly to the sandy soil, and wove them around each other into a circle. Adrien watched warily. I was excited at having stumbled upon this great pleasure from my girlhood, and for the moment my own anxiety and self-consciousness were stowed away. I pulled out more vines and wove them around the circlet, more and more until I had a thick green crown. He will like this, I thought, and I was surprised by the intense pleasure the hope of pleasing him gave me.

I studded the crown with clover blossoms and buttercups, and then it was done. I showed Adrien my handiwork. He smiled; his eyes asked a question. Yes, I said, it's for you, and placed it on his downy golden head and sat back, eager to watch his delight.

And for a moment he *was* delighted and reached up to touch the crown gently. But then I saw his gleeful acquisitive joy give way to betrayal and guilt and remembrance, and his blue eyes clouded with bewilderment before they darkened in anger. He ripped the crown from his head and threw it as far as his short arms could manage. I don't want it! he shouted. I hate it!

And that's when I started crying.

Somewhere in the back of my mind, in the untouched field where I assumed my atrophied maternal instincts dwelt, I remembered that I was supposed to be the grown-up in this situation, but I couldn't help it. A year's worth of frustration had been tapped, all my ragged attempts to entertain them, all the endless afternoons of fitful conversation and forced attempts at fun, all the cowed guilt and dumb animal shame, all of it came forward in this moment in which I realized how very much I wanted these children to like me. How much I liked them.

Adrien couldn't believe his eyes. He'd seen the impossible—an adult behaving as he behaved. And then his face softened; he understood. Incredibly, he understood. He got up and walked over to the discarded crown and tried clumsily to stick a few fallen flowers back. It's pretty, he said gravely. Can you fix it?

He sat in my lap then, and I breathed in the warm salty scent of his sandy head as I repaired the damage, and I can still feel the rhythmic swell of his small bare chest, the way the air stilled and the world came down to a small boy and a beating heart, the way I began again.

Chapter Seven

A MONTH LATER Lee lost his job as editor of the Style section. There were many theories as to why. A small element may have been the lingering distaste from the scandal we had caused, but for the most part it was his own doing. Editing the Style section called not only for taste and discernment but for a flexible diplomacy, something Shelby had managed with consummate skill. But from the beginning, Lee had stubbornly ignored the hints and suggestions emanating from Katharine Graham and others in the upper echelons of the paper, despite the fact that to do so was one of the less subtle forms of career suicide.

I had heard rumors of trouble and passed them on to Lee, but he dismissed them, and the tension tightened to the point where it was almost a relief when the blow finally fell. Bradlee offered him several other positions at the paper, but in Lee's eyes he had been fired, and he could no longer stay.

His colleagues watched in disbelief—Lee had always been so cautious, so methodical in his career; most of them could find no precedent in his character for the tone-deafness he had developed in Style and his refusal to descry the signs that were so obvious to everyone else. He had begun his career at the *Post* as a copy boy twenty-three years before, working his way up in the traditional manner, from night police to beat reporter, before making the longed-for leap to foreign correspondent. As an editor, he had picked his way deftly past cutthroat competition, cranky bosses, and balky reporters, a company man, reliable and consistent. There seemed to be no explanation for his current behavior beyond the cliché of the midlife crisis.

He had one close friend who saw it differently, however. He had been a colleague of Lee's in Vietnam, and years later he would tell me how Lee's departure from Style had reminded him of his reportage on the battlefield. "There would be incoming, very heavy, bombs falling everywhere, the rest of us would all run for cover, except for Lescaze, who stood his ground, notebook in hand. He never flinched. Maybe it was just that impeccable code of honor of his, which demanded that he take the same risks as the soldiers he was writing about, but it was a strange thing to do when you are a twenty-eight-year-old guy with a young wife and a bright future ahead of him. It was as if he just didn't care."

He never would flinch. His sangfroid was as much a part of him as bone and blood. This much I had sensed from the beginning. But it had never occurred to me that a tendency toward the self-destructive was a trait we had in common.

Falling in love is irrational; why this man and no other? Only later do the reasons become apparent, and they are surprisingly different from those that were obvious in the beginning. I thought I knew Lee and why I loved him—part of it had to do with him being the sane one, the rock to which I could anchor my shaky little boat. He was, more than any who had preceded him, the Other, the one I couldn't have, the lost father, the phantom talisman of warm yellow lights. He was the one who would parry all my fears, banish my doubts, who saw me as better than I privately knew myself to be and made me yearn to meet his expectations.

But these are paltry psychological truths. They didn't explain the sweet, sad beauty of him, the way he transfigured me. I began to understand that part of it only in the days after he walked away from the safety of the place in which he had worked for over twenty years. He was no stranger, after all, to the lure of taking chances. He had needed, as much as I ever had, to save his life, even if it meant doing whatever it took to blow it up.

Then I saw something I think he knew all along: that it was not our differences that bound us but the things we held in common.

Within weeks of his dismissal, Lee accepted a job on the foreign desk of the *Wall Street Journal*. We moved to New York at the beginning of October.

I had wanted to move to the city for years, but when the

time came, I was somewhat ambivalent. I had found a more comfortable place on the *Post*'s city desk, mostly because the young woman who ran it had made one for me. She was young and married and pregnant, clear about her responsibilities, and straightforward in her dealings. My polar opposite. In the beginning I was sure that she would hate me, that she could see me only as a lightweight, the chorus girl in a tattered boa who had fetched up on the schoolmarm's neatly swept doorstep. But that was the mirror in which I, not she, was looking.

Grateful for her patience with me, I tried hard. As a Style exile, I was meant to teach the younger reporters something about the differences between writing breaking news and writing less deadline-driven stories. "Right now some of the younger ones think that if they put the word *blue* in front of the word *dress*, they've written a feature," she explained. "I thought maybe you could help them develop a little bit of a voice without getting too..." She paused, embarrassed. I finished it for her. "Without getting too precious and turning into a prima donna?" She nodded.

To my surprise, I loved being an editor, struck by the unpretentious professionalism, the hard-boiled talk, and the frequent kindnesses of the other editors as they dealt with the daily flood of novices and neurotics who demanded their attention: "Jesus, kid, you're such a cunt, what do you think this is—*poetry*?" I heard one guy say to an inexperienced reporter, before spending an hour with him gently teaching him how to write a lede. Editors—stop the presses—were human.

Editing allowed me to see writing from an entirely different perspective, as words that had to be found and fixed and rearranged and occasionally coaxed into song, a medium for information, not a personal route to redemption. And writers who turned every story into a mystical event were, whatever their merits, a pain in the ass. Like the kid who breathlessly turned in a story destined for the front page of the Metro section a half-hour past deadline saying, "You'll love the way I wrote this; there isn't one verb in the entire piece!" Jesus, I thought, what a—my colleague's epithet was one of the few I never used, but my point of view was the same.

Lee and I packed up our things—it didn't take long. There wasn't much we wanted to keep, and the list of things to be abandoned included Elver the crazy cockatiel. We put him up for adoption through an ad in the paper, and the day before we left his new owners came to get him.

I had lingered that last day in the newsroom, editing a story that didn't need editing, watching as the huge room began to empty and the adrenaline of the deadline subsided. I had only one goodbye left to make. I headed toward Bradlee's office, but he was on the phone.

There was something different about the living room when I got home, and it took a minute to figure out what it was—the cockatiel's cage was gone. I walked over to the bare wooden table, still strewn with scattered seeds, my eyes blurring with tears.

Lee emerged from the bedroom, a half-filled box in his arms. He was aghast to find me crying. Throughout all the preparations for leaving, I had been excited, giddy, treating the move like a long-overdue adventure. And now I was red-eyed and in despair.

"It's Elver," I explained.

"I don't understand," he said. "You hated the cockatiel, remember? He was driving us nuts."

"No, I *loved* him," I wailed. "The way he puffed up his little cheeks so hard when he tried to make a sound. The way he always missed the thing he was trying to land on. The way he screamed at us in the shower, and the way he walked around the coffee table like a little toddler—"

"He bit everybody's toes when he did that."

"I know, it was so dear. And now we're abandoning him. He trusted us, and now we betray him like this."

I couldn't explain my grief to Lee; I didn't see that it wasn't the cockatiel I mourned. But Lee did. It's going to be all right, he said, and put his arms around me. We left Washington the next day.

All that first fall and winter in New York, I waited for spring. Everything would be better by then: I would have stories to write and friends to talk to and my ears would no longer throb with the angry wail of the city. I would be at home.

But spring that year was cold and mean and merciless, and the March wind blasted down the streets from river to river kicking up tumbleweeds of trash. I had imagined April green and mild, but instead it bore only the signs of an exhausted winter: the once brightly colored wool hats that the old ladies wore were now encrusted with dirt and reduced to a uniform gray, and the cheeks of the red-faced old drunks in front of the OTB office downstairs were so chapped and swollen, they had nearly swallowed up their watery eyes.

I had no assignments and no friends, except for Lisa, who, by way of encouragement, told me how as a newcomer to the city, she called her answering machine and left herself messages of good cheer. The days were long and vertiginous — I was in free fall without the *Post* behind me to shore up my claim to be a writer. I could barely pick up a phone to make a query or look for work.

Gradually it got better. I began to write small stories for magazines I had never heard of, then better stories for magazines I never read. And finally, occasionally, stories for magazines I had always loved.

I had finished just such a story, a profile of a ditzy but talented fashion designer, when the phone rang with an invitation to a party given by a young couple I was just beginning to know — Guy was a writer for *Esquire*, Sarah the editor of a teen magazine. She in fact had given me the first freelance assignment I had actually enjoyed: "How to Kiss a Boy." It would be a real party, the kind given not by Lee's friends but by mine.

Lee and I had come to a gawky stage in our love affair, its perimeters stretched taut by growing pains. In our new life Lee was the one with the money and the status; for the first time I could not support myself on what I earned, which meant that when I spent too much, it was his money I wasted, not mine. Lee loved working at the *Journal*, and he came home no longer scraped raw by the day's events. New York was home to him, and he had changed key effortlessly, playing the city's chords and variations with a practiced hand. But I was in a place for which I had no map. And sometimes, I thought, a place with no escape hatch.

In New York the thirteen years that separated us showed painfully at times. We knew no one in common. His friends, the men and women he had known since Vietnam, since Bangladesh, since Exeter and Harvard, were older and distinguished and moneyed. They drank moderately, most of them, eschewing hard liquor for the oenophile's more refined pleasures. They talked about foreign policy. Their children were grown, and their marriages were at that stage of companionable accommodation that was a great deal trickier than it looked. They were confident and unusually successful at what they did. If they were professors, they taught at Ivy League schools; if they were writers, I knew their bylines from *The New York Review of Books* or from the Pulitzers they had won. They glided through the book parties in Manhattan, the cocktail parties in Martha's Vineyard, like swans, all the mad paddling kept well below the surface, displaying above it only the kindly glance, the keen insight, and the graceful aperçu.

They were all very kind to me, but among them I felt like a kazoo in an orchestra—the younger wife, the midlife crisis—and I read their kindness as condescension. Which, occasionally, it was.

But the friends I was finding in the makeshift world of magazines were my age, reckless and stained as I was by a youth that had lingered too long. They were maddened by the now-or-never nature of their thirties, ambitious, self-loathing, unpredictable; they drank hard liquor, almost always to excess, and while they liked to drink, they liked other drugs as well. My scandalous past was met only with mild curiosity. They knew all about the kamikaze nature of love. Their unions were volatile, and the fevers that sent them out into the night were sometimes cooled in errant beds. Their talk was both clever and competitive, and they lurched through their self-made disasters with a certain noblesse oblige. One of the best of them spent an entire year watching cartoons on television, unable to finish a piece on Pakistan. No one found this particularly odd.

I ricocheted between these worlds. An afternoon of cucumber sandwiches at a Princeton garden party sent me hurtling back to a bout of all-night drinking at a rowdy bar. I was up for grabs.

Lee was a sociable man, despite his gravity and reserve. He was at home in living rooms where the talk centered on ideas, books, politics. He had been out of the country at the dawn of the Me Decade: the self-confessional mode of conversation was both alien to him and repellent. I, on the other hand, have always had a few close friends who knew more about me than my shrink and, behind them, a very high wall keeping out what I tend to think of as Other People.

Once, in college, a good friend had asked which I would prefer—to be immortalized as a character in a novel, or to be cherished as a friend for life. A character, I said, of course. And wondered why he looked at me strangely. I know better now how rare is the friendship that survives the careless cycles of affection and betrayal, the shifting nature of a patch of common ground that once seemed eternal.

One night, in one of our first public appearances as a couple, Lee and I went to a dinner party given by a retired State Department official whom Lee had known for many years. I could manage cocktail parties, where I could sail like a dinghy in Lee's wake. But dinner parties were a nightmare. That night I was seated next to a Pulitzer Prize–winning author who had been a hero of mine when I was younger and the ambassador from some small but probably very important African country. I was very nervous, and because I was nervous and like to drink, I drank too much. The Jack Daniel's made me long for a cigarette. The famous writer was smoking a cigarette, which was enough reason for me to follow suit. Besides, the cigarette was a talisman, a declaration of allegiance to my own self, and although I had officially given up smoking years before, I enjoyed the occasional trespass with the immoderate pleasure of the forbidden.

Late in the evening I looked down the table from the warm interior of some prolonged fit of liquor-enhanced laughter to see Lee's cold, unsmiling face. I knew that look. It was the one that said, This is not the Woman Who Loves Schubert's Quintet in C Major. This is the woman my first wife warned me about, the Tacky Little Floozy Who Will Ruin My Life. I dreaded the cab ride home.

Lee and I had a complicated negotiation where self-indulgence was concerned. In the beginning we both drank too much, so that was all right, but lately my tolerance for alcohol had diminished drastically. Now it was usually Lee who drank too much.

On the other hand Lee had quit smoking for good when Adrien was born, while I had quit smoking more times than I can count. The only way I maintained any abstinence at all was to think of myself as a temporary nonsmoker. Lee, however, had met me in my most successful nonsmoking phase. Therefore, when he saw me smoking, it was a tocsin, reminding him of his own self-destructive tendencies and his own doubts about me.

I sat cowed and ashamed during the frigid cab ride

home, but by the time we arrived, I too was furious. Didn't the occasional cigarette balance out the extra martini? Apparently not. My self-indulgence, my lack of restraint, he told me the next day when he was finally speaking to me, had disappointed him. I bridled. My own friends would have understood.

On the day of Sarah and Guy's party, I went for a haircut. It was just meant to be a trim, but when the stylist began to comb it into its usual decorous bob, I stopped him. I wanted something different, I tried to explain. Something a little more, um, messy. Not messy exactly, but...

"I know what you want," he said sagely, or as sagely as was possible for anyone wearing black lipstick, henna-dyed dreadlocks, and a low-cut leopard-skin tank top. "You want party hair."

I left the shop with a small hurricane attached to my head, thrilled with the tangled wildness of it. Walking past the strange shop windows of West 57th Street, catching sight of my new hair, I felt it coming on, that need to go into the night a different creature. I passed a chic, expensive boutique I had grown to love and decided there was nothing in my closet to match this mood.

In the boutique a salesgirl took me downstairs, where they kept the racks of racier designers. I left the dressing room with a tight bright green miniskirt that would go well with black stockings and high-heeled pumps and a new lacy black sweater designed to fall fetchingly off the shoulders. At the cash register the clerk asked for my credit card and a driver's license. She looked at the picture, taken in Washington two years before, and then she looked at me. "You've changed," she said.

The party was downtown in Sarah and Guy's loft in the Bowery, a venue unspeakably hip. It began late in the evening, and we arrived later, climbing grimy tenement stairs to the already crowded space. The air was thick with music and laughter and shouted fragments of conversation and hazy with cigarette smoke. Almost immediately Lee and I were whirled in different directions, devoured by the party's maw.

"I came to Carthage," wrote Saint Augustine, "and all around me in my ears were the sizzling and frying of unholy loves." I remembered suddenly what it was like to walk into rooms like this, flushed with excitement and the potential for mischief. The room was swelling with the tribal joy that feeds a party sometimes. Sex was in the air: beloved, old-fashioned desire.

Sex was different when you knew you weren't leaving, when it was no longer a sort of performance art. To my surprise, it was more foreign, scarier, sweeter than I could ever have thought possible. It was part of something deeper now, connected to a reassuring dailiness and a deepening understanding of the strange mix of familarity and mystery that each of us confronted in the other. But sometimes I missed the way it once had been: an exuberant incantatory dream, untethered to the real world, unencumbered by doubt and washed in pleasure. I missed that kind of lovemaking. How could I love Lee and still miss it?

A Rolling Stones song blasted as I threaded my way to the bar to get a drink. When I turned back to the party, a tall young man with a lopsided grin was looking at me. A neon-light sculpture pulsated in the blackness; matches flared in the darkness. The music grew louder. The tall young man and I began to dance, and I danced the way I had always danced: as a preening, a display, an invitation.

We shouted questions at each other.

"Who are you?"

"Who are *you*?"

Where do you live, what do you do, who are your friends here, everything, but one thing. I did not mention that I was here with the man I lived with, the man I loved. I knew I should, but I didn't.

I woke up late the next morning. Lee was gone, having already left to go to the airport to pick up the children. My brain was wrapped in a thick scratchy muffler, letting in nothing but the occasional memory of some incredibly stupid thing I'd said. The rest of me was as brittle as spun sugar—every move had to be plotted just so, or I would splinter into a thousand pieces. It was clearly necessary to rearrange the day, to cut back, retreat, hunker down, the way we did under our desks in the fifth grade, practicing for nuclear holocaust.

The hangover rendered many of my cozy plans for the

weekend impossible. The making of soup was out of the question, but spaghetti carbonara might be possible. Going outdoors was potentially life-threatening, but we were out of milk and you can't be out of milk when children are coming. I would have to go to the grocery store. Perhaps I could manage it, as long as I didn't have to attempt actual conversation with anyone. I finished a second cup of coffee and a half-pound of bacon—grease was always an effective morning-after ballast—and was just summoning the courage needed to leave the apartment when the door banged open. Adrien flew in; his sisters followed a discreet and dignified distance behind, their father treading in their wake.

It was better with them now. Alexandra, Miranda, and I had found common ground in shopping and exploring the city—they were the only people who knew less about it than I did. They were more comfortable with their father as well, but that road was still strewn with boulders. He tried too hard, desperate to win them, afraid they would never forgive him. He would buy them things, ask them questions about their lives, which were changing so fast and so far away from him. But they read his generosity as an attempt to buy their love, and his awkward questions as disapproval, convinced they could not measure up to his expectations and that he didn't care for them.

But with Adrien it was different. He was seven by then and often came up to New York all by himself on the shuttle, proud of his status as an unaccompanied minor. Then he would run into my arms as soon as he arrived, and I would swoop him up, thrilled every time to be greeted in the same glad way. His father's reticence and worries had no defense against this boy. Adrien crashed through the newspaper behind which Lee was barricaded and jumped on his lap, he made Lee skip down Park Avenue, he bombarded his father with questions: what if a giant clam landed on the Staten Island Ferry, what if I could jump over the Empire State Building, what if a purple pterodactyl flew past the sun, what if I just love you so hard all you can do is love me back?

Adrien noticed that I had my coat on; he wanted to know where I was going. I was grumpy and wanted to be alone. Nowhere, I said, just the grocery store, I'll be right back, you would be bored. He insisted on coming—Adrien loved an argument. I surrendered—there were too many words involved in arguing.

Outside, on West 23rd Street, the air was cold and wet, and the sky was thick with ashy-colored clouds, and the smell of urine and vomit wafted in great waves from the walls of the OTB. The old drunks looked even more lost and dazed than usual, and the old women hunched their shoulders against the wind as they clutched their purses and dragged their shopping carts down the street. I growled some complaint, wanting only to get the errand over with.

But as we walked down the street in the twilight, Adrien had a soft, faraway look on his face, and he was very quiet, an unusual state for him. What was he thinking about?

"It's like a dream," he said. "Like I'm awake but in this place where everything is special and different and not like ordinary. Do you ever feel like that?"

Yes, I said. Sometimes.

Adrien was most often a whirlwind, tugging at all his custodians to go faster than they cared to or demanding to be picked up or to be told a story. He was stubborn sometimes, and as rowdy as any little boy his age, restless, distracted, uninterested in school—drilling him on multiplication tables could convince anyone that learning arithmetic ought to be illegal. Like other children gifted with compelling physical beauty, he understood the power of his charm and the effect it had on adults. Sometimes we would smile at his transparent attempts to wield it in the service of a later bedtime or the procurement of a new Masters of the Universe character.

But he possessed as well a quality I've rarely seen in children or for that matter adults: an uncanny ability to uncover the heart of someone else's longing.

Adrien had opened up his father like a peach because, more than anyone else, he understood Lee—his wish to escape his own reserve, his need for the affection he could never ask for. He had always known. When Lee's mother had died, after a long, slow decline into the oblivion of Alzheimer's, Lee had stood locked in his sorrow, until Adrien, looking up at him, took his hand and gently patted it. Lee's voice broke every time he told the story.

I looked around, and maybe it was the hangover, and

maybe it was Adrien's unconscious channeling of my own need to romanticize, but suddenly that grim and dreary street was transformed: for a moment I imagined that there was music in the air, and the red-faced old men were throwing down their beer bottles and snatching up the old ladies and waltzing them down the street, past green and blooming trees, and I squeezed the hand in mine, overwhelmed by the poetry and the power of a little boy.

In the afternoon the rain came, and we stayed inside, all of us sitting on the floor playing a game that had started out as Sorry but had evolved into an improvised orchestra of silliness. Several of the pieces meant to march around the board were missing, and I had put together a motley array of substitutes—a toy soldier, a salt shaker, the top to a missing pen—all of which had developed, under the children's urging, their own extremely eccentric personalities. I loved these moments, when somehow it all worked, and the grievances were stowed and the girls smiled and Adrien laughed with glee at the sight of his father joining in the prattle, and I was the magician who had conjured it all out of a desperate hat. Such moments were still rare, at least when we were all five together, and when they did happen, I reveled in them and wondered at the happiness they gave me.

The phone rang. Lee answered it, handing it to me with a look I couldn't read.

It was the tall young man.

He was surprised, he said, when a man answered.

Yes. Well.

Your husband?

Not exactly.

The conversation stammered on for a while, lame, telegrammatic, his invitation to coffee refused without explanation. I hung up. Lee was looking at me steadily, bemused, but asked no questions. I anchored myself in his eyes, and the bubble of errant eros was suddenly discharged. This is what I want, I thought. This is who I am.

But the whiplash unsettled me, this seesaw between selves, the rooted one and the vagrant one, and I wondered how I would find myself if I could no longer wander at will. Sometimes I knew what I wanted, sometimes I knew only what I was leaving behind.

I never talked about this with Lee, though I think now he saw more than I ever realized. Back then I needed secrets. They were the guardians of my independence.

When I looked up from the phone, the children were waiting expectantly. It was, after all, my turn.

Chapter Eight

IT HAS ALWAYS BEEN the custom among the women in my family to mark any great ceremony with the last-minute manufacture of a dress suitable to the occasion. Almost any of life's landmark moments will do: baptism, confirmation, graduation, funeral. Either my grandmother or my mother—or myself for that matter—realizes a day or two before the grand occasion that she has nothing to wear—and again we are off on yet another breakneck race against time.

This time, however, we were going for an entirely new level of daring. At ten o'clock on a mild January morning my mother was making the dress in which I would be married eight hours later.

No one spoke. My mother sat at the kitchen table over the sewing machine, her head bent low, her face frowning in combative concentration. Tension raised her shoulders and tightened the muscles in her neck, as she guided folds of fabric past the jabbing needle.

The dress would be beautiful when it was finished, a full-skirted ivory silk with fitted bodice, long sleeves, each with eighteen handmade buttons and eighteen hand-sewn buttonholes. But any well-made dress is a time-consuming process, a wedding dress exponentially more so, from the cutting of the fabric to the final finishing touches. The halfway point comes when the skirt is joined to the bodice, and the dress begins to reveal the roughest approximation of its final shape. My mother was only now approaching that pivotal step.

I should have been alarmed, but I wasn't; an unfinished dress lent credence to my still-extant hope that the wedding itself was only a bizarre hallucination.

I was thirty-four when I married Lee, not a young bride but fairly typical for my narrow slice of the world: baby boomer, middle-class professional, absurdly self-referential. My kind came to marriage late and cautiously: in our twenties the idea of a long-term monogamous commitment, legal in the eyes of the law, was about as hip as a Tupperware party. As I got older, marriage began to look inevitable but not particularly inviting.

My friends who did get married looked like bungee jumpers leaping off a bridge despite grave doubts about the dependability of the knots. Years before, I had been an attendant at my friend Lisa's first wedding: the entire bridal party had taken Valium to calm their nerves, and we walked the aisle like palm trees swaying in a tropical breeze. The groom, the best man, and the ushers, on the other hand, looked buoyant, pleased with themselves, and remarkably excited. It turned out they were all on coke. Another bride I knew sat through the entire ceremony, too faint to stand. Later she said she had simply been too hot, but no one believed her. Marriage was scary, a form of drowning: my politics, my culture, my history, told me that.

But life with Lee overrode all the evidence and the arguments. One evening I stood in the kitchen of our first apartment in New York, beguiled by the redness of the pepper I was slicing, suddenly aware of the moment, knowing, the way you do sometimes, that even as it passed, I had locked it away in memory. I looked over at Lee, his head bent over a book in a chair just a few feet away. Chet Baker's trumpet filled the room. I had never liked jazz, but now my life was steeped in this music and all it signified, and I wanted the song that Baker was playing never to end. Life is paradox: the thing I thought would sink me had taught me how to swim.

Lee never proposed; a formal question must have seemed irrevelant to both of us. We simply began talking about the ceremony. Lee and I both knew what we wanted: something simple, civil, and out of town, preferably out of the country. Venice maybe, or Paris. I would wear something incredibly chic in navy blue or, possibly, red. Just the two of us, no family, no friends.

"Are you sure this is what you want?" Lee had asked. "It's fine for me, I've already done this once. But what about you? I'd like to think this will be your only wedding."

Yes, I said, it's exactly what I want. I hated big fancy occasions. We were wondering whether Venice would be too cold for a winter wedding when Lee stopped to ask a question. "Have you told your parents about this?"

The next weekend was Easter, and I went to Fairfax. I told my parents the news in the dining room, over the roast lamb. My father was pleased. "Marriage is an important step," he said. "Even if you've been, uh, enjoying each other for a while." Years later he told me he had said a special prayer of thanks that night; he had been convinced I would never settle down with anyone halfway normal. After my announcement he knew he wouldn't have to worry about me anymore.

My father offered a toast. My brothers made jokes. My mother passed the green beans. Was it really going to be this easy? No. She would wait until later, after the table had been cleared and the dishes had been done, after my father had said goodnight and my brothers left for their own homes, after we had watched TV quietly together until I stretched and yawned and rose from the sofa to get ready for bed.

"He's so old," she suddenly said.

"So what? I don't care."

Mothers and daughters talk in code. There is always a second level of meaning. I knew Lee's age and his children were not the real objection. The translation to her objection was this: the way we had fallen in love was not respectable and just plain wrong. I had stolen something that was not mine.

"I can't tell your grandmother you're doing this," she said. "It would kill her. She'd never let me hear the end of it."

"The end of which part? My marrying Lee or the being killed?"

"Don't you get smart with me," she said.

I flushed with anger. "I don't want to talk about it. That's all over, it's done," I said sharply, and ran upstairs to my room.

But it wasn't done. It never would be. A vein of shame still ran beneath my happiness in loving Lee. As she often did, my mother had only said aloud what had worried me from the beginning and would for a long time to come.

As a culture, we don't use words like guilt and shame much anymore. They are no longer emotions but symptoms of neurosis or depression. The idea of doing what is right has given way to the imperative of achieving personal happiness, a concept that would have stunned Elizabeth Bennet in *Pride and Prejudice* or Newland Archer, the hero of Edith Wharton's *The Age of Innocence*, who gives up the woman he loves for his wife and children. In the nineteenth century's cosmology of virtue, honor trumped passion every time.

As a child of the sixties, I should have found that notion

ridiculous but I never did. For years, despite the time and talk and reconciliation, the slowly accreting weight of our life together, I could not square the fact that I loved Lee with my conviction that I should have walked away. That what I had done was wrong, but it wasn't a mistake.

I never resolved that contradiction: disquieting, uncomfortable, unavoidable. Perhaps there is in every life an action, an event, whether great or small, that is meant to lie restlessly at the heart of who we are; if we're lucky, it teaches us how to be human.

The next morning my father asked what kind of wedding Lee and I had in mind. I told him about Venice. He laughed out loud. "You're kidding, right? You think your mother will let you get away with that?"

"Mom doesn't even want me to marry Lee."

"No, she doesn't. But that has nothing to do with a wedding."

He was right, of course, but it wasn't only my mother. I had not reckoned with my father's tremendous pride in his · ability to put on a good party. A wedding reception would call upon all his organizational skills, the minute attention to detail, the marshaling of resources that had marked his days in the Quartermaster Corps. He was not about to let this opportunity pass.

Lee and I did manage to retain control of a few details: the wedding would not involve a high mass in a Catholic church or a reception at the Fort Myer officers' club in Arlington. We compromised on the presence of a priest, choosing a Unitarian minister who would wear a white surplice but promised not to mention God in the service. The wedding would take place at the Cosmos Club in Washington, a place whose swanky cachet appeased somewhat my mother's idea of propriety.

But it was still many hours before that march down the aisle.

"Do you want some coffee, Dorothy?" my grandmother asked her daughter that morning.

"I don't care," my mother mumbled through the straight pins clamped tight between her lips. She meant that she would like some coffee but was unwilling to accept the offer in any way that would seem to acknowledge my grandmother's thoughtfulness. She didn't want her mother to think that coffee would adjust the scales of her grievances by even a millimeter.

My grandmother walked in her awkward sailor's gait toward the counter near the stove. The ham was out, and she clucked disapprovingly at its ragged shape, took a knife, and carefully scraped the cut end, smoothing out notches and tears in the flesh until it was pink and uniform and perfect. "See that?" she said to me. "See how much better it looks?" Then she wiped the countertop with a damp rag, her stockings rolled up to just above her knees, kept in place by the press of the papery-pale blue-veined flesh. Earlier my mother had suggested she put on some socks. My grandmother refused. "I don't want to look like an old lady," she said.

"You don't need to do that, Mother. I already did," my mother said to my grandmother, when she caught sight of the dishrag.

"All right, Dorothy, all right." My grandmother's harsh, raspy voice grated against the air, the voice that I have always loved. She walked heavily out of the room, determined not to talk to anyone until her ill treatment was acknowledged, or until her avid curiosity brought her back.

My mother and I exchanged glances. The wedding dress undulated across the table in great waves of silk. My mother was making buttonholes. I was working on the hem.

Mothers and daughters live in a matrix of emotions that blind insight and hobble love. They lose each other for a while, sometimes forever, each unable to see the person the other has become. Sometimes, though, an image crystallizes; the parts become a whole. I wonder, sometimes, in what frame Zoë will find my portrait. In the image I carry of my mother, she is sitting at her sewing machine.

It was, it still is, a green Elna, now fifty-four years old. State of the art when she bought it, the Elna was a mechanical marvel, capable of extraordinary powers, reliable in ways her family never was. She often said she would be lost without it, and I think she would have been. Sewing was the anchor to her soul; the long hours spent at the kitchen table, guiding fabric past the insistent needle, were the hours in which she could be completely herself.

My mother always said she made clothes because she could not afford to buy them, and when she was young, that was true. The clothes she made telegraphed her yearning for a prosperous, well-ordered life, set well back from the edge, like a teacup in a china closet. She dreamed of going to Harvard, even in the years when the five members of her family lived in a three-room apartment, when money was so scarce that the pennies needed for the trolley car could rarely be spared. The scholarship she won to the Parsons School of Design went unclaimed. There was no money for room and board.

Instead she put herself through night school and married a young lieutenant studying for his master's degree in engineering on the G.I. Bill. From the first assignment in Tokyo to the last at Fort Myer, she sewed all her clothes and mine. The cocktail dresses and tailored suits, the pheasant-feathered hats that swooped so elegantly at Sunday mass, my playsuits, and all the rest became a counterweight to the demands of marriage and motherhood, a promise made to the life she still hoped for.

Clothes became the key to our closeness; the dreams we wove around them provided an unselfconscious place where we could meet. Most of the time when I was growing up, my mother and I were locked into the dizzying demands of our precarious climb, my mother pushing me up to the ledge that would lead to the life she wanted for me, while I tried hard not to fall and wished for safer ground.

But we walked as fellow pilgrims among the giant bolts of fabric, so heavy she tottered a bit pulling them off the store shelf. She liked the stiff, unyielding ones whose very resistance testified to their quality. The fabrics had first and last names, like people: Moygashel linen, silk shantung, Forstmann gabardine. Even now when I hear them, they provoke a small jolt of iconic respect.

In the hushed groves of dresses in the department stores, Lord & Taylor, Garfinckel's, Woodward & Lothrop, we were co-conspirators, wandering sharp-eyed until the detail on a dress or the cut of a jacket drew our attention. Then I would keep watch, on the lookout for salesgirls, while my mother whipped out a tape measure and committed to memory, through repeated incantations, the width of a skirt, the depth of a pleat. The Roman Catholic catechism defines a sacrament as an outward sign of inward grace. That's what the clothes were, to her, to me.

Sitting at the kitchen table at the indomitable Elna, my mother was not merely making my wedding gown. She was recognizing that in my life an entirely new chapter, one in which she could have only a minor role, had begun.

We had found the prototype for the dress in the bridal salon at Bergdorf Goodman. We didn't buy it, of course. While Lisa kept the saleswoman occupied looking for alternatives, my mother measured, examined, exposed, and calculated every dart and seam while I, as always, stood guard.

My mother sent me upstairs for a piece of white netting. Until last night we had forgotten the veil, an absolute necessity in my mother's view.

"You'll never make it in time," my father said as I passed by. He had never been late in his life.

My mother's theory of time, on the other hand, was based loosely on the miracle of the loaves and fishes: if she needed more, it would appear. Even now she is completely baffled when the time runs out. For my mother, a deadline was always a gauntlet, and she rose with combative determination to the challenge. Dressed in curlers and a nightgown, she weeded and washed and ironed until the last possible moment, when, against impossible odds and in the middle of unimaginable anxiety, she would career desperately to the finish line. Her procrastination used to drive me crazy—it still does—but I understand it better. It was not only a personal revolt against the dictates of her husband but a kind of high in its own right, the dread mounting as the moments raced by, a deliberate provoking of disaster. It was essentially the approach I took to growing up.

Upstairs in my room I found my grandmother making my bed. We could smell the steam rising from the kitchen, from the pots of boiling potatoes and cabbage leaves. "You still like pierogies, Lynn?" my grandmother asked me as she smoothed down the sheet; she had heard of the strange things that made it into my salads these days. Yes, I told her, though I still couldn't make them. I had written down the ingredients and proportions, the techniques for kneading the dough and shaping the dumplings, a thousand times. But the recipes always vanished before I could attempt a solo flight. Besides I couldn't imagine anyone but my mother preparing them.

My grandmother watched me as I tried to help her make the bed. I tugged at the sheet in an effort to smooth it and instead managed to insert an extra wrinkle.

I waited for a scornful snort that didn't come. For a moment her implicit contempt for the incompetence of others was banked; in its place was a shrewd curiosity.

"So you're finally getting married," she said. "Why?"

Only my grandmother would ask that question. Life has left her derisive toward the pretensions of men and the stupidity of women. She married because that was what women had to do then. To her, I looked like a dolphin swimming willingly into the net.

How to explain?

The year before our wedding, Lee and I moved to the apartment in which I live still. It was hot, the end of July, and the day had devolved into dusty cardboard and bad tempers. In the humid high-ceilinged room, his elder daughter and I were unpacking endless boxes. Lee was at work; I regretted that I had no similar escape.

Alexandra was sixteen, and that day she was an emotional black hole sucking all the air out of the room. I was angry with her because she guarded her fury like a troll his treasure and because she wouldn't let me in, because our tongues were thick with unspoken words, because I had fallen in love with a man whose complicated network of love and obligation was now part of mine.

But I said nothing, and she said nothing, and side by side we unwrapped layers of newspaper from the objects within them. The first boxes had contained some of my things—record album covers missing their records, an ancient pair of cut-off blue jeans, the stainless-steel cutlery I gleaned from my mother. Paperback books with cracked spines and torn pages. Spiral-bound notebooks blank beyond the half-starts and broken promises.

The next boxes were packed carefully. They contained objects nested carefully in newspaper, some of it fragile and yellowed; things that belonged to Lee's parents, things that were only now becoming a part of my life, now that we had a place to put them.

A silver coffee service, gold-rimmed demitasse cups, a clock embedded in beautiful old leather. Cocktail hats, filigreed and feathered, cream-colored linens, a solid brass paperweight in the shape of a heart. A watercolor Lee's father had painted of the carnation he had given his wife on the day her only child turned sixteen. Elegant artifacts of a vanished era, the aching, accurate measure of the irretrievable past.

"I don't know where we're going to find a place for all these things," I said, mostly to myself.

My lover's daughter did not respond. She was inspecting a small ebony head that used to sit on the mantelpiece in her own house in Washington. She placed it on a recently un-earthed end table. It looked good there, she said.

People took care of things in the world of Lee's parents, in the world of mine; they kept them and polished them and placed them gently where time would do the least amount of damage as they acquired the rich patina of years. I under-stood then a little better my mother's own hopes when she got married, the ones she stitched into the clothes that hung in plastic garment bags in her closet. Maybe that was why I was getting married, because the time had come to recog-nize the past, to understand its connection to the present, its influence on the future.

That was not what I told my grandmother that morning. I talked about love, and she grew bored.

"Well, good luck, then," she said with a curious gallantry, as if she were offering a final cigarette to the condemned.

In the end it was a wedding like every other—it was a wed-ding unique to itself. At the hour when the ceremony was to begin, I sat in a dressing room upstairs from the waiting guests wearing only a white satin slip. My mother had been putting in the zipper when I left the house. When she was at last en route, she had taken a wrong turn on the Beltway in her panic and arrived an hour late. As I pulled the dress over my head, I cursed the day we decided that eighteen buttons that had to be fastened into eighteen buttonholes on each sleeve was a very clever idea.

I forgot my bouquet, and so did Lisa, my matron of honor. My father marched me up the aisle in military time, leaving the string quartet scrambling to catch up with us. Adrien, smiling broadly, stood with the minister at the front of the room. He was the best man; he held a velvet pillow on which rested the rings. Mine was new, Lee's had belonged to his father.

The food served at the reception resembled an international exhibit of world cuisine, with separate stations for caviar, sushi, roast meats, crudités, and of course pierogies. I barely saw Lee except for the ceremonial first dance, in which I stepped repeatedly on his toes. I danced a few polkas with my uncle and flew around and around the room with Adrien, neither of us having any regard for either the tempo or the tone of the music. My new stepdaughters both wore black. They told me later it was not meant to be a statement; their father had taken them shopping and said the color was perfectly appropriate. Adrien helped us cut the cake, still my favorite memory from the wedding.

My raucous Polish relatives and my taciturn New England

family kept a polite distance from each other, until the time when the formal photographs were taken. The bride and groom posed first with my father's family and then with my mother's.

"We're number one!" my Polish aunts and uncles shouted as if they were fans attending a fancy-dress soccer game.

And that night, when it was finally over, I looked at Lee, my husband now, and turned the word over and over, feeling its strange weight and gravity. Was a wife any more grounded in the world than a pirate? It would take years to learn the answer. I would only know that I was happy. I could love Lee in a different way now, without looking over my shoulder for the edge of the cliff. We had fallen off the cliff and landed safely.

Chapter Nine

A MONTH AFTER we were married, my new husband gave me bath towels as a Valentine's Day present. The towels were red, in honor of the occasion, and they were "seconds"—the kind with snagged threads or other flaws that consign them to the bargain shelves. He had taped a bow to the Macy's bag by way of gift-wrapping.

I cried when I unfolded them. I was furious: the towels transformed the comfortable dailiness of love into a romantic high noon, forcing an emotional accounting in which I found my husband sadly wanting.

I can't remember anymore why I was so angry, but my reasoning must have been something like this: I have staked everything on this man, and he is not what I thought. He is not the Man Who Cries When He Reads Ford Madox Ford. I have defined myself in terms of this choice, and this is the kind of man he really is, the Man Who Gives Towels.

Now I know that we were not really married then, that

we were still in teen-romance mode—he loves me, he loves me not—still riveted to the drama and pitched emotion of courtship and passion, in which a passing glance can detonate a crisis.

I smile now when I remember this story. For years after that Lee gave me bath towels on Valentine's Day, and every time I laughed. The gift, and my reaction to it, had become part of our story. But the laughter was its own edgy commentary on how the two people who smiled at the joke were indelibly stained with each other's expectations and disappointments, how the individuals we once were had been permanently changed by the life we lived together.

All marriages begin in myth, a carapace under which the real marriage takes shape. Since Lee and I had plundered one marriage to make another, our initial idea of romance yielded reluctantly to the reality of daily life. You do not break up a marriage only to argue over the dishes with the one who was meant to take you away from the dullness of arguing over the dishes.

Inevitably our myth began to crack. Privately, I think, we each pulled out a set of scales and began to wonder if what we had given up was worth what we got. There were nights when we sat at the dinner table with nothing to say to each other, and I remembered all the nights in restaurants when I had watched such silence between other couples with smug contempt, wondering how they got that way.

Eventually I would understand that there are cycles to

domestic life—times when you're in love; times when you coexist as amiable roommates, too busy to take much notice of each other as long as the domestic machinery is humming along; times too when the oxygen in the marriage becomes too thin to breathe. That's when the bickering begins: the sharp tone to the casual comment, the stubborn refusal to give in, are small declarations of independence. The arguments prevent smothering, like the holes a child punctures in the top of the lid to make sure the grasshopper in the jar survives.

One night Lee and I had an old friend to dinner. The subject turned to Chinese domestic politics, a subject about which I knew nothing, unlike my husband the foreign correspondent and editor on the foreign desk of two newspapers. He and I began to argue about a perfectly meaningless point of fact. We covered the same rocky patch of ground for several interminable minutes while some still-sane remnant of my character wondered why it was so important that I win this debate.

I looked over at my friend, the survivor of a cruel marriage and a crueler divorce. She was smiling. I asked her why. She said, "I just remembered why I'm glad I'm not married anymore."

Eventually, our fights became more fraught, grounded in a future circumscribed by the choices we had made. Usually the fight came down to children. The only time we had even touched on the subject before we were married had been in the fright-filled days before Lee left his first wife. "What about babies?" I had asked him before the decision became final. "I love babies," he had said. I didn't press him then. I myself was ambivalent, alternating between the conviction that I would ruin my life if I didn't have a child and that I would ruin my life if I did. Even after we were married, I sometimes wondered if I only wanted a baby because Lee had made it clear that he most definitely did not.

In June Lee went to Africa to report a series of pieces for the *Journal*. He would be gone six weeks. For the first time in a very long while I would be completely alone.

In the beginning his absence was simply terrifying. Without Lee in the apartment, I didn't feel at home. The loft was beautiful, but most of the things in it—the furnishings, the paintings, the books—belonged to him. His absence heightened my own lack of weight in the world. In the shallows of the night I lay awake, listening for intruders.

It was better at work. Having managed to make exactly no money as a freelancer, I had taken a job in the feature department of *Newsday*, a Long Island–based newspaper that had recently launched a New York City edition. But even there I found cause for concern. I wrote a weekly column about— actually, I was never quite sure what it was about; every week involved an anxious search for a subject, not to mention the by-now-shopworn concern of whether I was any good.

Worry became my second job: whether Lee was happy,

whether he was sorry he married me, whether he'd get Alzheimer's like his mother did, whether he'd be killed in a plane crash, what he'd look like when he went bald. Without Lee to countermand them, the fears pressed in, demanding to be heard, like feral customers at a gourmet grocery store.

My anxiety had nothing to do with any of these things, I see now. I was simply beginning to understand the ways in which my happiness was handcuffed to another's.

Sometimes I went shopping, often at odd hours. I cruised rug stores, linen departments, kitchen supply shops. There was a weird sleepwalking quality to this wandering, and the purchases I brought home one day—designer sheets, complicated slicing machines—were always returned the next.

Other times I found myself looking anxiously for things that were not lost: a pair of gray pants that turned up in the closet, a bracelet that I never wore but had to find.

I thought I was going crazy, not inspired-artist crazy, a romance that had fueled most of my single life, but neurotic-housewife crazy. I had forgotten how to be alone.

And then halfway through Lee's absence, something changed, as if I had shifted a psychic gear. Suddenly I was deep into adultery: I first noticed it one morning when, instead of pouring orange juice into a glass, I drank it straight from the carton, a habit I had concealed since I saw Lee wince when he caught me in the act. After that life became a series of gleeful delinquencies. I spent afternoons listening to Linda Ronstadt, a singer my husband hated, while knitting, an activity he found mindless. I took long walks in the soft summer rain, exulting in the fact that there was no one waiting for me at home, aggrieved and wanting dinner.

Robert Louis Stevenson wrote that after he was married, his private world disappeared into the eye of an unblinking observer who had the right to witness and judge his actions, follies, and foibles. He meant it as a comment, not a complaint. I missed Lee and longed for his letters, but without him around, I felt as if I were having an affair with myself. An innocent escapade, as these things go, but still a betrayal — of the person I was with my husband, the one who represented my half of the couple.

I'd met my old friend, the girl in my back pocket, the one who was irresponsible and unconnected, the one who was happiest in the hum of errant desire. She had been eclipsed by the mystery of marriage, and while most of the time I was glad to see her gone, there had been times when I missed her, and the hidden places where she lived.

Around this time I had a dream: a band of wild Indians, straight out of a fifties Western, galloped around the house, bare-chested and ululating wildly, hatchets raised. I ran, I thought, to barricade the door. Instead I let them in, and they stampeded through the living room and out the back way.

One day I received a phone call from a man I'd met briefly while working on a story in Aspen a few months before. At the time frantic about deadline reporting, I hadn't paid him much attention except for the information he could give me. Besides I had no real idea what he looked like—the story was about World Cup ski racing, and everyone was buried in wool hats and pillowy parkas. Now he was in New York and invited me to dinner, an invitation I accepted.

In life, John Updike wrote, "there are four forces. Love, habit, time and boredom. Love and habit at short range are immensely powerful. But time, lacking a minus charge, accumulates inexorably and its brother boredom levels all."

I had not been married long enough to discover these truths for myself, but others had. Once when Lee had been in Washington for the weekend, I went out drinking with some magazine friends, and the talk turned to infidelity.

According to the self-help books popular at the time, adultery was a syndrome like alcohol addiction, a plea for help, or merely outmoded, something people did before there was pay-per-view. My friends approached the subject from a different perspective. The question on the table, after a considerable amount of red wine, had been where, exactly, did you draw the line?

"Drunken kissing in a taxicab."

"An out-of-town one-night stand."

We were titillating ourselves, wondering what we would do, wondering which of us had done it.

Or whether we wanted to: the consensus among us was that marriage, when it worked, was both complicated and rewarding enough to make it a wholly engrossing way to live,

one worth the sacrifice of that first caress from a new and unknown hand. And yet there were times when the idea of having sex with one person for the rest of your life could make
your head hurt.

There was, however, a dissenter. One of the longer-
married among us insisted that he would rather eat an olive
than make love to a stranger. It was a sensible attitude,
though not a prolonged one—he later ran off with his secretary and took to writing sonnets about her pedicures.

I met my dinner date at a small seafood restaurant near
my house. Divested of hats and parkas, he was alarmingly
handsome: tall, tanned, and dark haired, with blue eyes and
a slow, shy smile. For the first time in years I hauled out the
old camouflage—taunting, flirtatious, argumentative.

When dinner was over, he walked me home. A little
alarmed at myself, I invited him upstairs. I made him tea,
and we talked—about my marriage and his divorce and
briefly about books—until he revealed that he was a devotee
of Ayn Rand, and I had to change the subject.

It got late, and I walked him to the door. His eyes asked a
question to which I had no immediate answer. He made an
oddly formal speech. "I just want to say that I'm really attracted to you," he said. "I thought you ought to know this."

There it was again, that rush I used to get, that sense of
basking in a man's attention, of coming fully to life. Then he
kissed me.

It was a warm, wet, sloppy sort of a kiss, his tongue thick

and stupid in my mouth. But that wasn't the deal-breaker. Lee trusted me, and nothing else mattered as much as that.

This moment at the door wasn't about love, it wasn't even about sex. It was no more than the exercising of an un-used muscle, just to see if I could still do it, like a middle-aged man still vain about his six-pack. I didn't want this guy at all, and the thrill of inviting disaster vanished. I landed safely back onto the bedrock of my marriage, and I was de-lighted, so delighted I smiled, a huge goofy grin in which there was, apparently, much room for misinterpretation: he looked a little disappointed when I said goodnight and shut the door behind me.

Lee came home a week later. He walked in tired, jet-lagged, haggard, carrying the same battered maroon canvas and leather suitcase he had always carried, seams ripping on the sides. The one he had brought with him to my apart-ment the day our lives together began. I was in his arms be-fore I knew it—I didn't want to let him go. I looked into his eyes, and yes, he was glad to see me too. We were both re-membering why we loved each other.

The next day, in the morning, when I made the coffee and poured my orange juice into a glass, I thought about the girl in my back pocket.

My truant self. It was confusing; Lee brought out the best in me—with him, I was kinder, more responsible, less neu-rotic—but I was more timid as well, less apt to discover the world for myself, deferring instead to his greater experience.

I was dismayed, thrown a little off balance by the contradictions between my married and solitary selves. I would have breathed easier if I had known what I know now—that the old anarchy and joy would always be there, feeding other rivers. But so much had to happen first.

I loved him, and I saw now that I loved the things that had begun to grow in our marriage: the dry wit and the dumb jokes, the quiet fund of conspiracy, the shared opinions and the private understandings. The restraint and tolerance that increased over the years: "Their eyes," John Updike wrote, "had married and merged to three." And finally, the occasional blinding beauty of another soul. Together they made all the hard parts worth the fight.

We drank our coffee, and Lee told me stories about his trip. As he talked about a taxi driver in Nairobi who gave him shelter one night and would accept nothing in return, his eyes filled with tears, and I thought about how much I loved him for it. He caught me looking at him.

"What is it?" The concern in his eyes belied the offhand way in which he asked the question. "Is something wrong?"

Nothing, I thought. Not anymore. "It's just that life is so much better with you in it."

Chapter Ten

ADRIEN HAD JUST turned eleven when he died.

In the last year or two he had begun to leave his childhood. He had grown thinner and taller and a little quieter, though still buoyed by frequent moments of spontaneous glee. The awkward self-consciousness of adolescence had not yet touched him. His sense of the ridiculous had kept pace with his growing up, and so had his uncanny understanding of those he loved, his precocious attention to the feelings of others.

I saw it in the way he balanced, with a watchmaker's precision, the abiding preeminence of his mother's love and his own puckish bond with me. He would call his mother every evening when he visited us in New York, lowering his voice to speak to her in soft tones only she could hear. And then he would come and nestle in close beside me on the sofa to watch whatever movie that night promised the greatest number of car crashes and thunderous explosions. I was touched that he would try so hard to care for us both.

That year he spent his spring vacation with us. The sweetness of those days knit them together in a long, easy dream. We didn't do much: long walks in Central Park, where he and his father tossed a football around, evenings spent going through his father's childhood collection of baseball cards — they were both fanatics for the game — or listening to Lee read *The Kid From Tompkinsville*, the story of a young ball player trying to make it in the majors, a beloved book of Lee's when he was a boy.

All that week he and his father were as silly as clowns together. Adrien still liked to make Lee skip down the street, and I would watch them, this elegant man and this beam of a boy. My job was to pretend to be embarrassed by this dreadful lack of decorum, and to be shocked at the very suggestion that I would ever do such a thing myself.

He and I would sing together. He adored "Joy to the World" by Three Dog Night, and we sang it at the top of our lungs, his steady soprano doing what it could to balance my off-key enthusiasm. He still jumped into my arms at full tilt; I thought about how sorry I would be when he was too grown-up to do that.

On his last day in New York, Adrien and I took a walk together, while his father was at work. We made plans for the summer as he scuffed along in his battered sneakers and grass-stained sweatshirt and the corduroy pants that were now too short for him—he was proud of that. He darted away every time he saw a pay phone he could check for change.

We ended up in Washington Square Park, crowded after many days of rain with college students and tourists, hucksters and ice-cream vendors. The fountain in the center shot high into the air. The wonder of the first warm day pervaded everyone—even the gaunt sinsemilla sellers looked less shadowy and wraithlike. Adrien wanted an ice-cream sandwich; he spotted a stand near the Arch. I took his hand and, before he could even ask, began to skip across the park. His face was pure astonishment.

A week later his mother called. It was a Friday morning, a strange time to be hearing from her. I was writing at home. Her voice was taut. She had tried to reach Lee at the office, she said, but he had gone out. Adrien had been in a car crash on the way to school. He had been helicoptered to Children's Hospital. He was unconscious.

When Lee called, I told him the news. Within an hour he was on the shuttle to Washington.

I went down the next day and took a cab directly to the hospital, hoping my presence would not be considered an intrusion. The waiting room was crowded with family and friends. Adrien's mother stood up and walked over. We embraced. "I'm glad you're here," Becky said with gallant generosity. "I know you loved him too."

Adrien lay in a criblike bed in the intensive care unit, wearing just a diaper, returned to the babyhood he had only recently quit. His body was pierced by tubes and needles, his head a turbaned swath of white that made him look like a pale young prince. One blue eye was half open, fixed and unseeing. From time to time his arms moved involuntarily in slow spasmodic arcs, as if reaching for something, then fluttered down, unappeased, to his sides.

For a week the days and nights passed in cruel hopes and spare comfort. Lee and I had been staying with close friends, returning from the hospital late at night and leaving early. But one night Lee decided to stay on at the hospital. I don't want him to be alone, he said. Dawn had barely broken when he called, hoarse, beyond words, to say that it was over. Adrien was dead.

We gathered around his bed with Becky, Miranda, a junior that year in high school, and Alexandra, a freshman in college. A young Episcopalian priest made the sign of the cross over Adrien's head. "Well done, oh good and faithful servant," he said. "May bands of angels bear thee to thy rest."

The morning of the memorial service, we gathered at Becky's house. Everyone moved cautiously, preparing food, making ready. I was desperate, in a way I had never been before, to be of use. Becky must have seen that. "Miranda can't find anything to wear," she said. "Would you help her?" I found her sitting on the floor in the basement, alone, as apart as she could make herself, nearly lost in the shadows. A thin light filtered from narrow windows near the ceiling. A jumble of black clothes surrounded her.

"Your mom thought you could maybe use some help," I said.

"Nothing fits. Nothing's right." She spoke in a monotone. She was barely there.

A black skirt emerged from the bottom of the pile, fairly unwrinkled, plain and somber.

"It's too long," she said.

"I think we can fix that," I said. "Wait here while I get a needle and thread."

When I came back, Miranda tried on the skirt. She stood while I knelt down at her feet and pinned the hem as evenly as I could, the way I had watched my mother pin the clothes she made for me. When it was finished, she put it on, and without a word we went upstairs.

National Cathedral, vast, brilliant, glittering, was filled to the brim that morning. One of the *Post*'s national reporters made a nervous joke. "There's more people here today than there were for Justice Black's funeral."

I looked around at the congregation, friends of the family, Lee's colleagues from the *Wall Street Journal*, and what looked to be the entire contents of the *Washington Post* newsroom. Some were friends, others I knew only by reputation and observation: a pompous TV columnist, a tyrannical editor, reporters from other papers. Some of them I had liked, a few I had made fun of, many others had humbled me with both their talent and their modesty. But that day such distinctions didn't matter; what did was the immense tangled net of them, the strength of that net, the weight it could support.

I saw now the arterial connections that pulsed between the men and women I had known only as disapproving judges of my petty dramas. I felt the fragility of their hopes, the nightmares that haunted them, the stalwart way they tried to stand guard against the random hand of history. I understood something I had not understood before: the terrible necessity of other people.

The Right Reverend John Walker, the Episcopal archbishop of Washington, presided over the service, assisted by two other priests and a canon. The choir sang. The congregation chanted Psalm 23, and the bishop spoke what words of comfort he could. An anthem was sung: "... *at thy coming may the martyrs attend thee, and take thee up into the holy city, Jerusalem. There ... mayest thou, with Lazarus, once a beggar, have eternal rest.*" Such lofty company for one so young. The music we heard as we left the cathedral was more appropriate: The song that had once been his favorite now painted a portrait of the young man he might have become.

> *You know I love the ladies*
> *Love to have my fun*
> *I'm a high night flyer and a rainbow rider*
> *And a straight shootin' son of a gun ...*

One of Adrien's teachers read from letters written by his classmates at the Beauvoir School. Peter Kann, the publisher of the *Wall Street Journal* and a close friend of both Becky and Lee, remembered the boy's boundless energy, his sometimes surprising turns of speech: "I'm as dry as Ethiopia," he once told Peter in asking for a glass of water.

But the only moment that mattered was the moment when Adrien's father got up and smoothed his tie and went to the lectern to give the eulogy for his only son. And all I know of courage was contained in Lee's voice when, at the end, he asked the congregation to rise, and to say his son's name out loud together.

Adrien.

Chapter Eleven

Back in New York, a few days after the funeral, Lee and I took the program from the memorial service to a nearby framing store. It was important that we go as soon as possible; Lee had to keep this one last thing safe.

We walked up to the counter, and Lee began to explain what he wanted; the paper trembled slightly in his hand. A big blonde in stretch pants shouldered her way past him. "What's the matter with you?" she said. "Can't you see I was here first? What are you, blind?"

I looked at Lee anxiously. He managed a small smile. "Well, I guess life really does go on, doesn't it?" he said. "I wasn't sure."

Outwardly the surface held. Lee went to work, came home, ate dinner, just as if these things still had meaning. It was hard for me: I couldn't imagine how it was for Lee. He was calm and kind to everyone who asked after him, and as understanding as ever toward the worries, large and small, of others. Once when he noticed me worrying over a story due the next day, he sat down and touched my cheek and told me what a terrific job I would do. His thoughtfulness in the depth of such sorrow staggered me.

For the first two months we didn't talk about Adrien much; it was enough to get through the day. But one morning in June I found him standing, just standing, in the room that had been Adrien's whenever he visited. It was early in the morning, on a Saturday, about the time when Lee would have been meeting him at the airport. Lee looked up.

"The paper didn't come today," he said.

"I wonder why."

"Because Adrien's dead."

He stood there unable to move, paralyzed by that one unalterable fact. The tears coursed down his face. "We had a common language," he said. "He was the only one I didn't have to explain myself to."

There was nothing to do but hold him.

We made love that night for the first time since Adrien's accident, not out of desire but from the need, I think, to find out if we were still alive.

A few weeks later I found out I was pregnant.

Lee and I had reached an impasse on the subject of having a baby. We each understood the validity of the other's position, but that had done little to loosen the knot of anger and resentment in either of us. Everything changed the night of the memorial service. The mourners had departed, and the spring sunlight had finally faded. Lee sat quietly in a chair in the living room of the friends who had cared for us from the beginning of the nightmare. He stared into an empty fireplace.

I came over to comfort him, but he spoke before I could. "Throw away the diaphragm," he whispered. "I was wrong to say you couldn't have a child. No one should be denied that happiness."

Even now I am overwhelmed by the compassion in those words and the love they expressed, that Lee could be thinking of me at such a time.

And now it had happened so terribly soon.

"Congratulations," he said, his voice unsteady.

"Is it all right? I mean, so soon?"

"Yes. Of course. But it's good that babies take nine months," he said. "It will give us time."

A few days later I called Lisa, my oldest and closest friend, and told her the news. The words "I'm pregnant" sounded incredible as I said them.

"What are you going to do?"

"What do you mean?"

"Are you going to have it?"

I was startled. There was no question, of course.

"Yes."

The sound of her crying came faintly over the telephone.

Lisa and I had met as rivals, when I was a sophomore in

college. I had fallen in love with a boy named David who had forgotten to mention that he had a girlfriend. Lisa and I had hated each other, of course. But when the dust settled, I was with David and Lisa was with David's best friend Rick. For reasons that made total sense in the sexual politics of the sixties, all four of us ended up living together for a year in Cambridge, arguing over whether the presence of David's hot dogs in the refrigerator tainted the purity of Lisa's macrobiotic seaweed.

The boyfriends had long since disappeared, but not a week had gone by in which Lisa and I didn't talk, and there was no event in my life that didn't become larger, more valid, after I had told her about it. When I got the job at the *Post*, there had been only one thing for me to do: fly straight to California, where Lisa was working on an independent low-budget feature entitled, appropriately enough, *Off the Wall*. We drove back East in Lisa's temperamental ten-year-old Volvo, our itinerary determined by the towns mentioned in a much-beloved Little Feat song: *"I've been from Tucson to Tucumcari, Tehachapi to Tonopah…"*

We left Santa Cruz with four bottles of Jack Daniel's, two grams of cocaine, and a Baggie stuffed with dope. We slept in a hot-sheet hotel in Las Vegas. Fought viciously while Lisa fasted on herbal tea and feasted on invective, forgave each other as we watched the sun rise in Monument Valley, heard the news that our latest lovers were cheating on us while the sand crept through the doorway in the old motel on the edge of an Indian reservation. Our days on the road were giddy, sun-washed, and we arrived in the East exhausted, with no drugs, no liquor, and no money in our pockets. I remember that trip with a sharp piercing pleasure, the arc of its exquisite, fragile flight.

She was my life raft and always would be. Once after some angst-ridden lover had left her, daunted by her headlong plunge into their affair, she shrugged and said, "I think that boy is happiest in the breakdown lane of life. Not me. Say what you will about me, and god knows I have my faults, but you'll always see me coming, honking my horn and driving my eighteen-wheeler straight down the middle of the highway." There was an indomitability about her, a vitality that never wavered and never would.

Most women I know have one friend who knows all your secrets; Lisa was mine. I've never understood how men get along without them.

Over the years Lisa and I had talked about babies. Did we want one? Maybe. Would it ruin our lives? Probably. We never strayed far from the fence. It was as if we had an unwritten pact to stick together one way or the other. Then Lisa discovered she couldn't have a child. In the sixties she had used the IUD known as the Dalkon shield, which was later withdrawn from the market when many women, one of them Lisa, developed severe uterine infections.

We didn't talk about it much after that, but I kept track of the time left before the choice was no longer mine.

Lisa and I had dinner. I was the second to arrive at the small vegetarian restaurant we had chosen. In front of her was a glass of white wine.

"This is excellent. You should have some," she said.

I hesitated, a little embarrassed. "I can't."

"Oh," she said, and as her face changed, so did the geography between us. "Right."

We talked for a long time. Lisa was in the process of making a successful leap from freelance film editor to forming her own production company, but had doubts about the man she was seeing; she envied my rootedness. I talked about my worries that a baby meant the end of my career and my independence; I envied her options. We looked at each other a little sadly. "I feel like there's such a huge canyon opening up between us," she said. "I worry that I'm going to lose you."

"It's not a canyon. More like a small crevice with a bridge over it. I mean, we both still have terror, intermittent self-loathing, and raging insecurity in common, right? We can be a tag team. When I'm missing being single, you can complain about the perfidies of men. And when you wish you had a nest, I'll tell you about temper tantrums and diaper rash."

At my first appointment at the obstetrician's office, I was handed over to the nurse practitioner, a strong, solid Russian woman named Maya. She was crisp and grim, like a Marine Corps drill sergeant addressing a raw recruit. I would have amniocentesis. I would not go to the dentist or take a sauna—"unless you want to boil the baby." She looked at me as if that were a distinct possibility. No sit-ups. No exercise of any kind.

I asked about running, and she said abolutely not. And then, "How old are you?" I told her. Thirty-seven.

"That's too old. You should have had this baby when you were young."

The doctor, a handsome dark-haired woman about my age, concurred. "We don't recommend it," she said stiffly when I asked about the running. "As a matter of fact, we don't recommend any aerobic activity for an elderly prima-gravida."

"A what?"

"It's the term used for a woman having a first child late in life. It's considered a high-risk pregnancy. In any case, it's never been shown that exercise is at all beneficial to the fe-tus. It's only good for the mother."

I found another obstetrician, a man well into his sixties who asked me only one question.

"Do you want this baby?"

I was surprised by the confidence with which I said yes. Absolutely.

That was true. But the joy I felt came accompanied with a kind of guilt, irrational perhaps, but there nonetheless. My pregnancy was a betrayal of Adrien. And of Lee. My excite-ment over the baby felt unseemly and wrong.

One night, very early on, I had a dream. The baby materialized from my belly as if to introduce itself. It was a girl, with grave blue eyes and long brown hair, parted in the middle. I asked her if she was all right, and she nodded. I'll see you later then, I said. But when I woke up, I was shaken. I would not have a girl, I would have a boy, with blond hair and blue eyes. It had to be a boy.

Now it seems obvious that I was trying at least in my fantasy to replace Adrien, to take away the emptiness in Lee's eyes. But I didn't understand then, and my seeming preference for a boy worried me. Would I be disappointed with a daughter?

By mid-July I had a bit of belly (you've popped out nicely, my doctor said) and enormous (these things are relative) breasts in which I took great pride. I took a walk through Washington Square Park, in blue jeans I could barely button and a black T-shirt. I felt earthy and voluptuous, like Anna Magnani in *The Fugitive Kind*, ready to give birth to a dozen children.

I walked past the fenced-in toddlers' playground, trying to imagine the day I would be there, listening to the laughter of my own perfect child. Lost in thought, I nearly collided with an exasperated woman about my age struggling grimly to soothe a wailing whey-faced baby dressed in an excessive amount of pink. The woman looked grim, angry, and unfathomably tired. Anna Magnani disappeared. Mommie Dearest took her place. Was that what I would also become?

As soon as I got home, I went straight to the closet and hauled out my ancient brown leather bomber jacket, for years the symbol of me at the peak of my fantasy self. I couldn't zip it closed. I thought about all the women I knew who talked about their lives before babies as if it were a long-forgotten, nearly mythological era. I remembered how Elizabeth laughed when I brought up some adventure of ours from our early days as young single women. "It's funny," she had said. "I can't even remember who I was before the baby was born."

The next morning I went to the hairdresser. His wife was pregnant too. "So what shall we do today?" he asked, as we both stared into the mirror. "I love working with pregnant hair," he said. "It's so thick, so shiny. How about growing it longer so we get the whole madonna thing going?"

I told him to cut it short. Very short.

Lee watched as I undressed that night. "That's an interesting look you're evolving," he said. "From the neck up you're early George Harrison, and from the neck down you're pre-Columbian fertility figure."

"Do you still think I'm pretty?"

"Of course I do. It's just different now. You're old pretty instead of young pretty."

"*What?*"

"You know, pretty in a matronly way."

I burst into tears.

·   ·   ·

One weekend in July Lee and I invited a couple we knew to the beach. They had an eleven-month-old daughter. I was excited to have a real-life baby on the premises, to see what our lives would be like.

Jonathan and Marjorie, the baby's parents, were long-time friends. He was a soft-spoken, thoughtful magazine writer, one of the gentlest people I had ever met. She was a TV news producer who dressed in vibrant colors and an artful mix of new and vintage fashions. At least they had been. The couple we met at the train station, barely visible under the small mountain of luggage and equipment, bore only a faint resemblance to their former selves.

Marjorie was dressed in ill-fitting jeans and a stained T-shirt, her hair a kind of wild thicket around her face. Jonathan had a wide-eyed, haunted look.

At first glance, when seen safely contained in her father's backpack, their daughter Anna was Gerber-baby perfect— apple-red cheeks, china-blue eyes, a chubby face wreathed in smiles. Once liberated, however, she turned diabolical, caroming off the coffee table, hurling small objects to the ground, coating every available surface in baby drool.

The parents meanwhile were transformed into maniacal marionettes, jumping every time Anna cried, turning her bedtime into an Olympic competition. "Let me do it," Marjorie said, jumping up from the sofa. "I can get her to sleep in three minutes flat."

"I don't need your help," Jonathan snapped. "I've done it

in two." He disappeared into the bedroom with the still-screaming Anna.

The next morning we went to the beach and spent an interminable hour setting up a resting place for the baby that could have doubled as an emergency operating theater. Anna cried nonstop, a reasonable reaction to her parents' efforts to care for her. Jonathan stuffed her into sandy denim overalls because he feared a chill. Margie removed them two minutes later. When the baby finally did fall asleep, Marjorie began to cut her fingernails. Anna howled. "What the hell did you do that for?" Jonathan roared. Still quarreling, they took the now-hysterical baby back to the house.

I walked down to the water's edge where Lee had taken shelter from the infantine storm.

"What is it? What's wrong?"

"I've ruined both our lives."

At the end of the summer we went to Martha's Vineyard. The trip had become something of a ritual over the last few years. We stayed as guests of an old friend of Lee's who lived in Paris now and his beautiful volatile French wife. Every summer they rented the same house on Menemsha Pond, and throughout their stay the place overflowed with old comrades—a novelist Lee had admired since their shared experience as war correspondents, a well-known law professor with a dazzling wit, and one of the founders of *Liberation*, the radical French newspaper. That summer Lee found a sanctuary there. We spent long days on a private gated beach, not far from the one my friends and I had camped on illegally during college, and I listened half-asleep to conversation that alternated between serious discussion and badinage as precise as a tennis game.

Alone on the beach one day, I picked up one of the fish egg sacs—a skate's, I believe—that lay scattered up and down the beach. It was hard and black and spiny. I thought about walking on that same beach with my son or daughter by my side. I thought about this ancient cycle of procreation, random, blind, and mutable, and how it had devolved improbably down to me and, soon, mine. I thought about Yogi Berra. As he used to say, "Who'd a thunk it?"

As the weeks went on, as my belly swelled, and I became to myself more visible than I had ever been, I became, at the same time, invisible. On the street men's eyes slid over me as if I had the sexual appeal of a mailbox. I could look at the world without the constant awareness of being looked at; it was one of the first great gifts of pregnancy.

My condition was becoming more real for Lee as well. On one of the last warm days of the fall, we took a walk through Central Park. The pathways were crowded and the lawns full of people sunbathing. On a patch of grass outside the Met, a sandy-haired boy tossed a baseball high in the air, then ran to catch it in a glove that was old and burnished with time, the kind handed down from an older brother maybe or a father.

Lee watched for a long moment. "I was wondering," he said hesitantly, "what we say to the baby when...we're sad about Adrien. How do we explain?"

"We'll tell the baby all about Adrien," I said. "And the baby will love him too."

One day in November the wind turned and the season changed. I spent the day buying impossibly small things for an impossibly small person I had never met. Who was this amiable if reticent companion, so much a part of me now, soon to be so separate?

I made dinner that night, listening to the Doors, wondering about the baby, born into a different world, one in which the Doors were merely elevator music, not an erotic call to arms. I thought about the hurts he would suffer, the ones she would inflict, and the cataracts of grief, disappointment, and despair I was setting in motion.

"I am opening up cataracts of grief, disappointment, and despair," I said to Lee when he walked into the room.

"No, but you're turning into one," Lee said wryly. "It's the hormones. One day you will be amazed to remember that you cried over sappy TV commercials."

Toward the end of the pregnancy, friends and, for that matter, strangers on the street unleashed a barrage of uninvited information about what was about to happen to me. *You'll never sleep again, you'll never wear silk again, you'll never finish a book*...the talk irritated me, mostly because I was afraid it was all true.

"Did you find yourself feeling at all, well, ambivalent while you were pregnant?" I asked Cynthia, an old friend from the *Post* with two children of her own.

"Oh, yes."

"How long did it last?"

"It was still happening when they wheeled me into the delivery room. I wondered if it was too late to change my mind."

One cold night in January I began to dance. It was late, and Lee was away at one of the many dinners I used my pregnancy to avoid. Cole Porter was playing "I Get a Kick Out of You." Something lifted. Something settled. I took off my clothes and feasted on the sight of my body, the heavy belly, the thick pubic hair, the dark line that ran up to my navel, the reddened nipples, the fulsome breasts. The music caught me, and the sense of effort that had accompanied the last few weeks, the slowness with which time now passed, all left me, and I was light and happy, and I danced through the empty apartment as giddy as I have ever been. The books said that I would know I was about to deliver when I developed a powerful urge to organize, to make right the nest, and I had waited for what would be, for me, an entirely novel instinct. Obviously the baby wasn't coming anytime soon, because all I wanted to do was dance.

My labor began the next morning.

.   .   .

The pain was slow and rhythmic at first, each contraction an iron band tightening slowly around my belly, not unwelcome, not unbearable. A birthday present: I turned thirty-eight that day. Lisa took me to lunch.

Things changed quickly. Soon I found it hard to tell the end of one round of pain from the beginning of the next. By the time I arrived at the apartment, I could barely walk. Lee came home, and we took a cab to St. Vincent's Hospital. The driver had said nothing on the way until I pulled myself out of the backseat. Then he looked me up and down. "It's a girl," he said.

All night long we waited. The baby's amplified heartbeat filled the room until the sound of it and the sight of the meters on the machines started to fuse with the memory of Adrien's hospital room, where blinking red numbers brought only bad news. I couldn't bear it and asked the nurses to turn the sound down, to make the meter face away.

At dawn I was wheeled into the delivery room. They told me to push, but there was nothing to push with, no strength. Lee told me to breathe. I told him that if he said that one more time, I would have to strangle him. I heard nothing after that, I was so deep inside myself, nothing except for a strange animal moaning, a deep unrecognizable guttural appeal. "What is that?" I said.

"It's you," Lee said.

And then at last my daughter arrived.

Lee cut the umbilical cord—a ceremonial snip, as if it were a red ribbon at a public works project, and all I could think of was John Lennon's falsetto imitation of the Queen Mother in *A Hard Day's Night*, "I now declare this bridge open!"

At first I knew only that I was still hurting, great waves of pain that would not stop. Then I heard the first weak wailing cry, and my heart wheeled.

Is she healthy, is she whole?

Yes.

The nurse placed the baby on my belly. A red, wrinkled thing with tight-shut eyes and a strange cylindrical head.

I felt too weak to hold her, and so Lee took his daughter into his arms, walking slowly and silently around the room. I could only imagine what he was feeling.

That night the baby stayed in the nursery so that I could rest—nothing had prepared me for what had just happened, the violent change in body and soul, the pitilessness of a process that, once begun, was as uncontrollable as flood or fire. I tried to sleep, but the hormones surged and I came without touching myself, wincing at the pain I'd set in motion. I eased my angry body out of the hospital bed and looked out at the city and the cold starry night, spent, joyful, terrified, exploded.

When I slept, I dreamed of Adrien. He was lost, and I had found him. In one dream I found him in an airport, in another on a grassy hill. In each dream he was older, and the places I found him were farther and farther away. Grief is implacable, demanding its place among the living, not to be denied; that is the first lesson it teaches.

A few days later three of us entered an apartment that only two of us had left. I lay Zoë in my old bassinet, newly bedecked in eyelet lace and ruffles, a gift from my mother. That first night at home, my baby still looked like she had gone twelve rounds with the young Joe Frazier.

Within a week I was haggard with fatigue, and except during a life-saving visit from my mother, I stayed that way for weeks. I couldn't sleep. I read countless baby books, convinced I would make some terrible mistake. Whenever Zoë was quiet in her bassinet, I would jump out of bed to make sure she was still breathing. I stood there swaying, unable to leave, touching her tiny chest.

Lee watched me, worried. He wrote little poems and left them around the apartment, gentle and light, meant to fill my sails when they were luffing, as he said in one of them.

His own dance with his new daughter was a quiet thing, one of late-night walks and wordless comforting. What did he think about in those endless circumlocutions of the apartment? Did he think about the son he had lost, the wife he was losing? I didn't ask. I didn't know how to be married now that I was a mother, just as I didn't know how to be a writer, or a woman for that matter. There were no boundaries left, no private place where I could run. I didn't know where I ended and Zoë began. Where did you write from? Where did you make love from? The books didn't say.

The world shrank to just the two of us. My connection to Zoë had a love affair's tenderness, its violent pendulum from ecstasy to despair, its physicality, its wild unsteadiness.

I felt guilty about my absorption in Zoë, that what I gave to her I was taking from Lee. I could see his loneliness in his eyes. "I'm getting lost," I told him. "I'm losing you." He smiled in a way that acknowledged the truth of what I was saying. "I miss you," he said simply. "But I know you'll be back."

She was my mirror, my love, my ancient implacable enemy. In the morning I would fall exhausted and resentful to the floor, after spending a half hour trying to get her out of her Snugli. But then, in the afternoon silence, in the winter light slanting through the bedroom window, I would touch her lips with strawberries, and she would smile. In the evening, when finally the milk had come in and she could feed until she was sated, her face would glow like a small pale moon, her lips swollen and red-ripened, the milk blister still wet and pulsing, her mouth open like a drunken sailor's, and I would look at her until I drowned.

When Zoë was just six weeks old, my mother brought my grandmother to New York to see her. She stared at Zoë, finding her on some level incredible, as if the baby were a doll come to life. She was the only one in the family who thought

Zoë looked more like Lee than me, and I loved her for it. "She looks like she dropped from Lee's eye" was the way she put it.

The next morning she was up early, and I made coffee. My grandmother was quiet at first, lost in thought in a way I had never seen her. Her face changed. She began to tell stories, the stories she would never tell me before when I asked her, summoned from the past she had tried so fiercely to dismiss.

We sat on the sofa, three women and baby, all of us barefoot in our nightgowns. Now I heard about the father who drank away his paycheck, and the mother who suffered his beatings and his betrayals, of the glass factory where she went to work when she was twelve, of the snowy perfection of the napkins in the restaurant of McCreary's department store, a place that looked liked heaven to her, the place in Pittsburgh where she worked when finally she ran away from home at fifteen. I had never seen her cry before.

My daughter brought me these memories, all of them a part of who I was, drawn from places I had never been able to find before.

When Zoë was seven months old, I tried to get her to sleep through the night. She had been going to bed docilely enough, but now, the moment I put her down, she would start to wail piteously. I would come back and comfort her and put her back in the crib, at which point the whole cycle would start over again.

This was very bad, said the books. She was old enough to

sleep through the night. The books were very clear on this. Choose a night to make your stand, and stick to it. When the baby cries, ignore her. Put a pillow over your head if necessary. The crying will stop after a few hours, and in the morning you will have had a good night's sleep and helped your child to become a model of self-reliance. Screw it up, and the consequences will be dire—loss of self-esteem, a lifelong lack of independence, a fearful neediness that will enrich the bank accounts of psychiatrists yet unborn. Even worse, I would have failed the test and proved what an incompetent mother I was, that I wasn't really a mother at all.

That night I put Zoë to bed, determined to let her cry herself back to sleep. Alexandra was visiting us; I offered her a bed far away from the forthcoming drama, but she chose to stay on the futon near Zoë's crib, out of solidarity, she said.

Everything was quiet for a couple of hours, and then the crying began. I closed my eyes and put the pillow over my head, but I could still hear her. I listened for a while, waiting to feel the lurching wave of exhaustion and resentment that the cry usually triggered in me. But this time it didn't come.

Instead, I got up and walked over to her crib in the darkness, softly so that she wouldn't hear me. She had pulled herself up to standing: the sight of her on two feet startled me. She looked at me gravely and I looked back, and for the first time I saw her, saw my daughter. How little she was, and how alone, there in the night. What a large task was ahead of her, this life that she would negotiate, this world she would have to find her way in. How hard it was to be so little and alone. Suddenly it didn't matter what the books said—what mattered was giving her what I knew without hesitation she needed. I picked her up and sat in the rocker and held her while she slept until the first gray light of dawn.

Lee was out of the country for a few weeks, but he called the next day to see how the challenge had been met.

"We didn't meet," I said. "We didn't even shake hands." I told him what had happened.

"But what about what the books said?"

"They're just books."

"Good for you," he said. And then: "By the way—how has it been with me away, at night, I mean?"

Lee had always been extremely gentle about my fear of being alone in the dark, never making fun of me, offering suggestions from time to time on what might make it better when he wasn't there—soft music, a night-light, white noise. Nothing worked. But when he asked the question, I was surprised at the answer: "I'm not afraid anymore."

"That's wonderful," he said. "What happened?"

"I guess Zoë did. She can't have a mother who's afraid of the dark. I need to tell her the monsters aren't real."

Zoë was nearly two. She rose from the bed, infant Aphrodite in the tangled sheets, naked, shining, and proud. She walked on long spindly legs that emerged from the white cotton bubble of her playsuit, slapping red leather sandals against the pavement. She watched the sand sift through her fingers on a warm and windy summer afternoon. The way she said "flower" broke my heart. I folded the memories carefully away, against the years to come.

Friends said she took after her mother mostly. But sometimes, as she slept, or when she was taken by surprise, I would see it suddenly, the phosphorus of her father's character, his gravity, his tenderness, glowing in her face.

Lee wove himself into his daughter's life through stories. One Sunday afternoon he called out from the other room, "What does Dis mean?"

"The Roman god of the underworld," I answered promptly. Lee did the *Times* crossword puzzle in ink in about twenty minutes, but he had never taken Latin, and I always loved the chance to show off when there was a reference he didn't know. "He's mentioned in the *Aeneid* and, I think, the *Inferno*."

"I mean when Zoë is saying it."

I walked into the room. The two of them were sitting on the floor, and between them was a small farm all made of plastic—a barn and an animal pen, the requisite cow and horse and pig. Zoë was pointing at the horse: "Dis?"

"I think that means, what is this," I said.

"Ah." He turned back to Zoë. "This," he said, "is a horse. His name is Simon. He is a great scholar, an expert on ancient Rome, but I'm afraid he's very forgetful. One evening he forgot to close the door of the barn, and the animals all wandered away."

Zoë frowned. "Dis?"

"That's Lola, the cow. She's extremely vain and was once lured to the big city by a treacherous pig who promised to make her famous."

"Dis?"

"Now, that is Genevieve, a beautiful heroic chicken..."

We weave our love for each other out of stories. Sometimes they are stories others have told: I remember a man and a woman who fell in love over a novel. But the best are the ones we tell each other. Listening to the two of them, I would see Lee's stories take root in Zoë, informing her humor, her sense of irony, her wry eye ready for the foolishness and folly the world would unfailingly supply her. I think she will have less trouble understanding her own story because of the stories her father told her.

An autumn afternoon: Zoë was home with her father and her half-sister Alexandra, deep in the televised agonies of the Redskins. I had left to do the errands, the dry cleaners, the supermarket. It was getting late: I stopped to buy a pizza, thinking with pleasure how surprised they would be. Rounding a corner, I nearly collided with a couple in close embrace.

He was a young man with longish brown hair pulled

back from his face. The girl was about his height, and her hair was also long and brown, rendering them reflections of each other. He tilted her face up toward his, and she leaned back against the wall. He smiled as he bent to kiss her; her hands rested lightly on his hips. They had gone to a place I once knew well, but now could barely remember, an island unencumbered by doubt and washed in pleasure. I walked on a little faster.

A few weeks after Zoë was born, I had taken a mirror to see what I looked like, to see what had happened to this place out of which my daughter had emerged. It was, after all, a terrain I had known well—there had been a time when the inspection of one's own vagina (in the name of understanding our bodies without the interference of the medical profession, I think) was something of a feminist ritual. Now I was shocked by what I saw in the mirror. It was changed beyond recognition, reconfigured, by the tearing and the stretching and the contractions, into a completely unfamiliar landscape. "Will it change back?" I asked my obstetrician at my six-week post-partum visit.

"You've had a baby," he said. "This is how you are now."

This is how I am now: it is a cold December night, and I am giving a dinner party for Lisa in honor of her fortieth birthday. She arrives a couple of hours early. "I wanted to get here before the others," she tells me, "so that we can get all glammed up together."

I look down at what I'd put on, its suitability determined solely by its lack of milk stains or strained carrots. I look at her and remember how important dressing up used to be, the lacing of the gloves as preparation for adventure, the magical powers the clothes conferred.

Lisa notices. "It's not the same now, is it?" she asks.

"No, it's not," I say. "I came home from a party last week and realized I hadn't flirted with anyone. I'm not sure I remember how."

"I think it's like riding a bicycle," Lisa says. "You never really forget."

I wasn't sure. At that point I hadn't found a way to reconcile the young woman I had been, with her delight in courting chance, and the mother I'd become, with her urge to preserve, to connect. More and more the past was something that embarrassed me, as if I had to disown the girl I'd been to ensure the reality of the woman I had become. There had been so many masquerades. Was this just another, the middle-aged mother: earthbound, rooted, the one who found heaven in her daughter's face? Which one was real?

The answer, as the painter Joan Mitchell knew well, was both.

Mitchell was a painter who thrived in the New York art scene of the fifties, one of the few women to hold her own among the crazy, wild, and brilliant men who dominated the world of Abstract Expressionism. She herself was a hell-raiser, a loud and argumentative woman, a scene maker, a passionate lover, a mean drunk. And yet her paintings are deeply meditative, thoughtful conversations between a questing soul and the mysteries of shape and color. About a year before she died, she was asked about her brash public persona and how it related to her work. "There were always two of me," she said. "There was big Joan and little Joan." Big Joan, she said, was the one who went out to knock down the doors and put up a fight. Little Joan was quiet and shy and liked to stay at home. "Big Joan took care of little Joan. She made it safe for little Joan to stay home and paint."

Joan Mitchell was sixty when she said this. It takes a long time to understand that the girl you once were, the one guaranteed to fuck up your life, was also the one who saved it.

Just before I turned forty, I went back to Harvard for the first time since I graduated. I was writing a magazine story about the students there, specifically about what it was like to come of age in 1992, twenty years after I had graduated. I had had to force myself on the plane, afraid of what I might find—not among the living but among the ghosts that walked alongside.

The cab let me out in Harvard Square and I walked through a Cambridge I barely recognized, the shiny new boutiques and eateries a translucent presence over the bones of the past. Harvard Yard was bleak in that frozen period between the Christmas holidays and final exams; memory brought a rush of the same hollow anxiety dazing the faces of the few students walking by. The Yard was nearly empty and the tattered announcements and flyers tacked to the trees and buildings slapped and rustled in the wind. I stopped to read them, curious to know what had replaced the attempts to stop the war, to save the world, the incitements to riot, the provocative demands on behalf of both Dada and the dialectic.

The environment to which these new manifestos testified was a grim one: the flyers announced meetings of suicide prevention crisis counselors and child abuse support networks, seminars on date rape and pamphlets on safe sex, twelve-step programs for abusers of alcohol and drugs and food and credit cards, for the unlucky in love, for the lonely survivors of a thousand different variations of an always precarious adolescence.

For the next few days, I simply did the reporting I had set out to do. The girls I met were cautious, and angry that caution was so much a part of their lives. "It's different for us than it was for you," said a dark-haired girl who reminded me of Maeve, my roommate freshman year. "We know all the ways to say no, but we don't know how to say yes."

The boys I met were confused. They knew the girls were angry, and they sympathized, but the girls were also beautiful, and danced in their dreams.

Together they envied the gay activists, particularly the

young men for whom sex was a political cause, who fucked themselves silly in the name of equality, a strategy that sounded very familiar.

"These days ecstasy is out of fashion," Ellen Willis wrote in her essay "Coming Down Again." "It's become conventional to trivialize, if not condemn out of hand, the romance of sex and drugs that carries so much transcendental baggage. Yet the power of the ecstatic moment—this is what freedom is like, this is what love could be, this is what happens when boundaries are gone—is precisely the power to reimagine the world. We can't live in such moments, but we need them to make sense of our politics and our lives."

I listened, the veteran of now mythical days, which had given birth to the very pragmatism we had the luxury to disdain. This generation would have to reinvent love, I realized. But then, didn't we all?

On my last day in Cambridge, it finally became official. I was forty. I tensed, waiting for the wave of dismay and despair, but in its place was a joy, smooth and shapely as a warm stone. I thought about all the uncertainty and doubt and the tremendous drama the young have to deal with, the liquid thing identity was. I had survived my youth. It was good news; there was someone who needed to know it.

I went for a walk, to find the person I'd really come to see.

The day was cold and windy, the sky gray and heavy with rain. Icy puddles lay in wait at the curb. I touched one gingerly with the toe of my boot. I braced myself—for what?

And then I remembered: I was waiting for the cold shock of half-melted snow on a warm wet sock.

Sophomore year was the nadir of misery: the freewheeling joy of freshman year had been overwhelmed by an epic loss of confidence. I wasn't smart anymore, the admissions committee had made a terrible mistake. I sat in the back of classrooms in which I was often the only girl, unable to speak, and stared at notebooks as empty as the day I had bought them. I grew thinner because I couldn't eat when people were looking, and when I went to the library to try to catch up on the work I knew I couldn't do, I slept the afternoons away in large leather chairs. I walked late to class along these same cobbled streets, and in my haste I would plunge into icy puddles, and the shock of the cold would tell me once again what a hopeless case I was, a girl who couldn't even buy herself a warm pair of shoes. I had the money; I had the time. But the act of buying shoes was simply beyond my ability to take care of myself.

The cobbled streets led me, one after another, to the girl I had been, the one who listened to Mick Jagger and painted the walls of her dorm room black, who read *Love Story* when no one was looking.

I had forgotten her. How frightened she was, how little she believed in herself, how much she had needed the façade I had built for her out of arrogance and theatre and nerve. But walking along the Charles River, remembering the many afternoons I had sought refuge there, I finally saw her as she had been, sitting on the bank, knees up, arms wrapped around her legs, hunched against the cold, worried that this was all she would ever be. Poor thing, I thought. You were a beautiful heroic chicken and I should have loved you better. In a whisper I told her the amazing news: she was going to be all right.

Chapter Twelve

LEE FIRST NOTICED the pain late in August, when he sat down to drink a beer after a hard-fought tennis game: a shooting fire at the base of his spine.

He played tennis every Tuesday evening in the summer, a standing date with an old friend. They played outside, on the public courts, a ritual that began as soon as the days lengthened and the light lasted long enough to finish a match.

Lee mentioned the pain when he came home that night. That was unusual; he rarely took note of any physical discomfort. I said, "You should call Dr. Ruden."

He flicked his eyes in a way I knew well, signaling a firm intention to dismiss the advice out of hand.

"It's nothing." He smiled indulgently and left the room to shower.

In the world of our marriage it was high summer. I was working at home then, writing for magazines, better ones finally.

Lee was intrigued by a new assignment at the *Wall Street Journal*, and Zoë was a glorious five years old.

A couple of weeks later, in September, the three of us took a bus to a lodge in the Adirondacks, a massive Victorian pile that looked to Zoë like an ancient castle; the first night we spent hours making up stories of the terrible deeds that had been done there.

The next day we had signed up for a group outing, a scramble up a nearby rocky ledge. Zoë was very proud; children were supposed to be at least seven, but the leader of the hike had made an exception for her. We walked gradually upward through a humid dappled forest until we reached the first challenge, a tumble of rocks whose passage involved a short but intense vertical climb. I went first, then Zoë, then Lee, ready to help her if she slipped.

But when it was his turn to climb, he cried out in pain — I had never heard him cry out like that. He couldn't even move out of the way of the other hikers — it was his back, he said. The man behind him looked exasperated and said something to his wife about out-of-shape weekend warriors.

"Fuck you!" I said, furious. "How dare you?" Lee looked at me, startled.

We made our way slowly back to our room, and Lee lay down on the bed. "I'll be fine, I just need to rest," he said. He sent us off to paddle around the lake.

But when I came back, the pain had not let up. "I'm calling the doctor," I said. This time he didn't protest.

It's nothing, said our doctor in the city. Probably a muscle spasm or a slipped disk. When you get back to the city and the pain has subsided, have him come in and we'll take a look.

We had to take a car back. Lee couldn't sit up—he needed to be flat on his back. The next day I took Zoë to school and went to the offices of a magazine I wrote for. I was supposed to be researching a piece on the state of American marriage but hadn't yet figured out a way into the story. I was staring at the wall thinking about what to make for dinner when the phone rang.

It was Lee. "I'm sorry to bother you," he said, "but the pain is unbearable. Literally." He paused the way you do when the full meaning of a well-worn phrase becomes clear to you. "Could you get a prescription for me?" His voice was strained, almost unrecognizable.

The pills didn't work. A few days later I called an ambulance to take Lee to the hospital. A doctor there admitted him. "We'll keep him here, do a couple of tests, and get the pain under control," he said. "It's probably just a disk."

The doctor called the day after Lee was admitted. He said he had the results of the MRI.

"Why don't you come to my office?" he said. "We'll go over it there."

"That bad, huh," I said with a nervous laugh.

He suggested I make an appointment with his secretary.

·   ·   ·

There was nothing wrong with the disk. The source of the pain was a tumor that had wrapped itself around Lee's spinal column. There were a number of different possible causes. They would know more after a biopsy.

I was sitting with Lee in the hospital when the doctor walked in with the results. His face was tight-set, but the eyes told you everything.

"I take it you have news," Lee said. He was in less pain after some serious medication, but he couldn't walk.

"I'm sorry," said the doctor. "It's cancer."

He continued to talk, but the words seemed to be streaming out of the air itself, filling my head. The tumor on the spinal column was a secondary tumor, the doctor said. They were looking for what he called the mother tumor. It was probably very small, too small to have been detected earlier, but now it had metastasized. The tumors were growing and would continue to spread.

"We think the mother tumor is in the lung," the doctor said.

"Would you please stop calling it that?" I said.

"We need to do some more tests."

"What is the"—we both fumbled for the word—"prognosis?" Lee asked.

The doctor looked down at his charts. "Well, we can't really say. You never know."

"Can you stop it?" Lee asked.

"Possibly," the doctor said. "It's always possible." But he was looking down at his chart as he said it.

"What do we do now?"

What they would do first was radiation, the doctor said, to shrink the tumor, which would enable Lee to walk. They would know more when they had done the biopsy.

After the doctor left, Lee and I looked at each other.

"Bummer," said Lee. I had to smile at the perfectly inappropriate word he had chosen to describe an unspeakable situation.

The doctor had held out some hope that it might not be cancer, it might be some rare form of tuberculosis, but in the end they found the tumor, a microscopic spot on the lung. The oncologist we talked to said he would see Lee as soon as he was able to walk.

A few weeks later Lee was able to leave the hospital. We took the elevator down and walked out the front door to the corner to find a cab. Lee spotted one, a block away. We were standing at a tricky intersection at the center of several convergent streets, but if we crossed over quickly enough, we would be able to snag it.

I waited for Lee to hail it, because he was always the one who hailed the cab, just as he always walked on the outside of the street, nearest the curb. That was the way it was between us, one of the small negotiations that define who you are to each other.

But the cab was coming fast. Lee had his hand out, but he could not cross the street quickly enough to get the driver's attention, and after a second I ran with my arm up to the other side and the cab stopped. I waited for Lee to cross the street and then opened the door.

We looked at each other, bewildered.

That's the way it happens. You walk into a room, and when you walk out nothing is the same, and you know that it will never be the same again. It was true when the phone rang about Adrien, it was true when we left this same hospital with our newborn daughter, and it was true the moment I, not Lee, ran into the street to hail the cab.

The specialists all said the same thing: the cancer was in its penultimate stage of progression. There wasn't much to be done. The tumor, wrapped as it was around the spinal column, was inoperable. Radiation would help the pain, chemotherapy might stall things a little, maybe a lot. There was no way of knowing.

For a few months, life returned to a semblance of normality. Lee went to work every day. The *Wall Street Journal* could not have been kinder or more supportive. The editors offered him a car to bring him back and forth, but he refused, continuing to take the subway. Eventually he took with him an old polished walnut walking stick that had belonged to his father. People were less likely to shove him out of the way, or rush past him on the stairs, he said, when they took note of the cane.

Lee was determined to live as if nothing were different, as if he could beat the disease by ignoring it the way he would a garrulous drunk at a party. He worked hard and spent the evenings as he always had, playing with Zoë and reading the always-growing pile of faxes from the office, rough drafts, newspapers, books. I meanwhile buried myself away in books about cancer and kept track of the medical appointments, taking notes, making calls, and fending off the advice of well-meaning friends—sharks' teeth, you must give him sharks' teeth, you must try faith healing, meditation, fairy dust, always with the implication that if I didn't, his death would be my fault. I took a weak consolation in the rough justice of this nightmare: if this catastrophe had had to happen, then it was only right that it happened on my watch, given the upheaval in which our life together had begun.

Lee found it hard to talk about what was happening to him; if the cancer were just a chore involving lists and appointments and things to do, then maybe it would have no reality of its own.

And there was a lot to be done: radiation treatments, chemotherapy appointments, blood tests, white counts, CAT scans, a catalog all too familiar in the lives of too many. For a while shielding Lee from as much of the bureaucracy and record-keeping as possible provided me with a refuge from my own concern.

Autumn turned to winter. Lee's appetite disappeared, and he grew thinner. The chemotherapy had no effect. He began to work more at home, to save his strength. The regimen of pills he needed to take increased. I kept them in a red plastic compartmentalized box, labeled with the days of the week and the times of the day, and kept them refilled according to a chart I had made to keep track of them all, an endless rainbow of pills, the purple Prilosec capsules, the small white Dilaudid, the five-pointed Decadron, the large white Bactrim, the quantities and frequencies increasing relentlessly.

Zoë knew her father was very sick and that the doctors were working hard to help him. Once he cried out in pain so sharply that Zoë came running into the room frightened.

"It must be very scary to hear Daddy yell like that," he told her. "But sometimes grown-ups get hurt too. I don't want you to worry; it's already starting to feel better." She nodded and said nothing.

Still, we tried to keep life as normal as possible. On New Year's Eve Zoë and I went out to buy champagne. The streets were crowded with people shopping for last-minute party supplies, to celebrate the coming of the new year. I hated them. It was impossible to look into the infant year without already dreading its teeth and claws. Where would we be in a year's time? How changed? Last year at that time my father was alive—six weeks later he was dead. My mother would spend this New Year's Eve alone.

When we got home, Lee was cranky and irritable, scolding us for the length of time we were gone. I grew snappish in turn, something I could do with impunity when he was healthy, leading now only to a prick of guilt at my lack of patience. Early in the evening we opened the champagne. I tried to look festive, but the effect was ambivalent at best—blue jeans and athletic socks, a moth-eaten lace-edged shirt and a silk kimono Lee had given me one Christmas long ago. He wore his dark red pajamas and a very old Mets T-shirt.

Lee gave Zoë a small glass of champagne and brought out the video camera as he did on every holiday to mark the occasion. I was appalled by the bleakness of the scene and left the room to compose myself. But then I heard the sound of his slippers shuffling across the floor, his legs too weak now for him to lift them completely, and I started to cry. He came into the room behind me. "Have I done something wrong?" he asked.

"Yes," I said. "You got cancer." And I hugged him, gently so as not to hurt him.

That February Lee and I took a vacation in Puerto Rico. It came together almost as an afterthought: Zoë had wanted for a long time to visit her grandmother in Virginia all by herself. We decided to go away as well, taking advantage of a short interval between radiation and chemotherapy.

I found a place on the island that was small and quiet and relatively stair-free. Our room had a terrace at the water's edge. There were no tennis courts or sailboats to serve as cruel reminders, and no children whose boisterous play could prove a threat to fragile bones.

We had looked forward to the trip with a kind of hunger, a break from the long skein of hospitals, needles, and bad news. But at the hotel it became clear that the recent round of radiation had done little to relieve the pain in his legs and that there were new sources now, in his shoulders. To see him walk slowly down the length of the pool, his thin legs poking out of his trunks, to help him painfully maneuver the tiled steps that led to the restaurant cuffed me again and again with the reality of how fragile he was.

And watching him die was harder there, in part because I was undistracted by the hum of chores and the web of dailiness at home, but also because I couldn't help thinking of the way things had been when we had first visited the island, in the early days of our life together.

We had been new to each other on that earlier trip. Since then, though I had always loved him, there had been times over the years when I had confined him to the fringes of my heart, days when I walked the streets wanting only to be solitary again. Time wasted, I thought, as we sat together on the beach, and I hated myself for not having loved him as well as he deserved every minute of every day. It was impossible to see, as I made my sad accounting, how little those fluctuations really mattered.

From the beginning, Lee had been my witness, my warden, my liberator, my true north. He had become the element in which I lived. That had never changed. It never would.

In March Lee went back into the hospital. He could no longer walk and the doctors wanted to try and get the pain under control. He was there a few weeks, and for a time, he shared the room with an old man who was also being treated for cancer.

I would come in the afternoons and read to him, or watch him while he dozed. One afternoon the old man's wife was there when I arrived. The two of them were arguing about who was supposed to call his sister. "I told you to call her."

"No, you didn't. You never mentioned it."

"You never listen to me."

"I just thought it would be better for you if you called."

"Me? You were thinking of me? Since when have you thought about me?"

There was something oddly reassuring about their voices, small and querulous in that stern white room, their argument the campfire that kept the wolves at bay, a barricade against the moment when one of the voices stopped.

The next day the doctor gave Lee the news. There was nothing more they could do for him. He left unsaid what he really meant, that now it was only a matter of time. Lee looked up at him quizzically. "But I want to get better," he said.

At home he sat in his wheelchair, sometimes reading,

sometimes dozing, his large beautiful head bowed down to his chest. When he woke up, he berated himself for needing so much sleep, for not being able to work harder. "I wonder when it will get better," he said, and I knew then that he had not understood the implication in the doctor's words.

I said, "Maybe it's not. Going to get better."

"Why don't the doctors suggest anything new?"

"Because, darling, there is nothing more they can do."

He stared at me. His voice trembled with anger. "Then I should just go out in the street and die."

"No. But I think you should be more selfish about the time you do have. Try not to work so hard."

"But what will happen to you? To Zoë and Miranda and Alexandra?"

"We'll be fine. Please don't worry."

He wanted to know how long he had to live.

The doctors say it could be months.

But not years?

No, not years.

The look on his face left me without words or thoughts or even breath.

We will all die a different death; Lee's dying was of a piece with the man himself—brave and blackly humored, stoic, private, unblinking.

I was bossy, full of suggestions. I wanted Lee to talk about what was happening, to him, with me, and with his daugh-

ters. I wanted him to write to Zoë, a letter she would have after he was gone. I wanted him to choose the mementos he
wanted his daughters to have, the objects that were special to
him. And he wanted to, he said. But he couldn't do these
things, and finally I saw that to do them was to acknowledge
the horror that was happening, and that to acknowledge it
left only surrender. And so he clung to the skeletal normalcy
that was still left to him, a normalcy predicated on the idea
that he had all the time in the world.

I had always admired Lee for the understanding he
brought to what it meant to be a man; a large part of that understanding rested in an almost courtly attention to obligation. To take that away was to take away the man himself.
Still he could not always keep the reckoning at bay. Once I
looked up from the book I was reading to see his eyes fill
with tears.

"What's happened? What's wrong?"

"Nothing," he said. And then, "We had a good life,
didn't we?"

"Yes, darling, we did."

"We were happy, but I didn't always know that. I wish I
hadn't worried so much about the future. I wish I'd understood how lucky we were."

Zoë was in preschool during the week, but when she
came back in the afternoon, she would sit in the bedroom
and draw pictures for her father. She could only touch him

gently; even the pressure of her sitting on his bed was too painful for him, so she would lean over and touch his cheek or hold his hand.

She knew he was very sick and that we didn't know if he would get better. But like her father, she kept much of what she was feeling to herself.

One day he asked me to call her into the room.

The walls nearest to him were covered with the get-well pictures she had made for him, crayon flowers, smiling faces, and many varieties of animals wild and tame. The pictures were taped at the top and rustled slightly whenever the sheets were straightened.

"I've tried very hard to get better," he told her. "But now the doctors don't think I will. They think I won't live much longer."

For a long time they looked at each other.

"I'm sorry," Zoë said.

Lee's eyes filled with tears. "I'm sorry too."

She stood next to him holding his hand until he fell asleep.

We lived in a kind of limbo that spring. There was a hospital bed in our room now, but neither of us slept much. There were medications that had to be administered around the clock at two-hour intervals. The hospice offered help, but Lee wanted no one else to care for him, and I was quick to agree, seeing how much of an invasion of privacy it would be for this most private of men.

We worked out a careful system to get him from the bed into his wheelchair in the morning. Lee put his arms around my neck, and I would take his ankles, and we would do a tricky pivoting maneuver where I slowly swung his legs around and straightened my back to bring him up to a sitting position; I was always tense and fearful because sometimes I did it wrong and I would bring pain to his left leg where the tumor had grown on his hip. After he had rested for a moment, we used a polished wooden board provided by the hospice to bridge the distance from the bed to the wheelchair, having adjusted the bed height so that it was just slightly higher than the seat of the wheelchair. He would hoist himself onto the board and inch his way over to the seat, and then I would restore the foot and the armrest to the chair and wheel him out to the living room. The first time we managed it, we felt like frostbitten explorers who had finally managed to plant our flag at the top of the world.

Lee's dreams became more vivid. Dreams of war, set in Vietnam, in Nazi Germany, in which he was the last man into the bunker, his experiences as a young reporter revisiting him in nightmare form. Sometimes the dreams were hard to shake off, and when he awoke, he would look around as if to get his bearings, trying to remember where he was.

One balmy evening in June I walked home from Zoë's

school. I had gone to the parent-teacher meeting that marked the end of the term. There was something encouraging in the unremarkable rumpus of the city, and I slowed my steps, taking it in: the young woman furious with her embarrassed-looking boyfriend, the off-key renditions of "Mr. Tambourine Man" under the plane tree in Washington Square Park, the man dressed like Zorro shouting out the same soliloquy on his ruined hopes, even the impatient braying of the taxis.

When I got back to the apartment, Zoë ran to me shouting, "Mommy, come quick, Daddy's gone crazy." I smiled at the exaggeration, thinking that maybe Lee had had a surge of energy and was playing some sort of game with her. But when I saw the frightened eyes of the babysitter, I hurried into the bedroom.

Lee was trying to stand up out of his wheelchair. He was agitated, his face contorted in rage. "There are robbers in the apartment, they're stealing the paintings," he said. The babysitter was in on it, he told me. She was the one who let the robbers in. He didn't know who Zoë was.

I tried to soothe him, thinking how apt a metaphor the theft of the painting was for how his life must look to him now, stolen right from under his nose. He looked at me incredulously.

"You're in on it too, aren't you?" he said. "You're trying to destroy me." He shook his head violently when I said I would call the hospice. "They're in on it too. You just want them to drug me up, so I won't know what's going on." I tried to leave the room, but he followed me in his wheelchair to make sure I didn't place the call. Along the way he pointed out the vanished paintings, still hanging on the wall.

Finally he stopped in the middle of the living room. "We have a problem in our relationship," he told me.

"What would that be?" I said.

"Let's talk. It's 1996, right? And we're in New York City, right? Well then, I'm sane. Now, if you're right and I'm hallucinating, then in the morning all the paintings will be here, but if I'm right, then you've been lying to me, betraying me, and I'd say that would be a problem in our relationship."

The phone rang. It was Alexandra. In a whisper I asked her to call our family doctor, figuring that Lee might trust him more than the oncologists at the hospice. In the other room I heard Lee shouting, "Mom, Dad, they're stealing all the paintings!"

A few hours later the hospice sent over some Haldol, a drug guaranteed, the nurse said, to knock Lee out for the night. Lee was calm for about an hour, but after that he was awake and with terrifying energy tried desperately to get out of the bed. He no longer distrusted me, but he was convinced that if he stayed in the bed, he would die.

The next morning an ambulance took him to the hospice, where he would stay while the doctors figured out what was going on. When I got back home, I tried to sleep, but it was impossible. I would like to say that I was wracked by pity for what Lee was going through, but at the time what I felt was rage.

I remember the fury though now I hardly recognize myself: I want to remember it, I need the sharp edges it displays. The past can sink so easily; at times only the sadness and the gentlest of memories are buoyant enough to remain on the surface. What happened becomes a fiction, when you want desperately to keep the reality with you always.

I was a mad thing that June evening, pacing through the apartment, concentrating all my willpower on preventing myself from smashing everything in the house. It was glorious to be so angry, as if a great tornado were sweeping through me, plowing through all the months of fear and patience and drudgery, uncovering all the small accumulated griefs of marriage. I was angry with Lee for getting cancer, angry at the cancer for what it was doing to him, angry that I had acquiesced when Lee asked that no outsider come into the house to help me care for him.

"I hate you," I screamed. "I hate you I hate you I hate you!" I said it over and over again, and I didn't know who I was saying it to. I could not differentiate among the images that crowded in: it was all the same, Lee, the doctors, my father, my editors, my self, my stupid self, until finally the storm stopped and I was so weak I could barely make it to the bed.

"You are going to go through one hell of a guilt trip when

you wake up," I said to myself, and then I slept for the next twelve hours.

Lee stayed in the hospice a week. The doctor wasn't sure what had caused the hallucinations; could be the pain-killers, could be the cancer spreading. His blood pressure was low, and he was weak and very drowsy. But his will was fierce. In his room, while he slept, the doctor and I talked in whispers about what was happening.

"It's either a virus that will pass, or it's the end," the doctor said.

Lee's voice startled us. "It's not the end," he said. "I want to live."

Lee's daughters came to stay with us. Both of them had grown closer to their father since college. They were magnificent throughout those long last weeks and, like their father, unflinching. They kept watch at night in the hospice, and when he was back home, they handled his wasted body with stoic tenderness, as they went about the endless work involved in tending to the body's most prosaic demands.

I had known them since they were girls, and I had watched them grow into the young women they were now. Fathers and daughters are always mysteries to each other; the mystery doesn't vanish when the dying begins. As they helped him select the music he wanted to be played at his memorial service, they had some of the same questions about him, about themselves, that they had always had. But to see them bear witness, to face fate in all its ambiguity, was to know what it means to become fully adult.

Lee's energy level and moods swung wildly, and they took it all in stride. The illness could make him restless, cantankerous, demanding, and it magnified the most frustrating parts of his character, for me, for them. He had a mania for organization on some days, wanting to catalog his music collection or rearrange his bow ties, and this they would do endlessly, trapped and miserable, watching the precious time they had with him be squandered.

But on other nights his mind would clear and they could be close; Miranda came home rain-soaked and exhilarated one night from the hospice because she and her father had read poetry together all evening. Encouraged, she decided the next day to read to him again. A close friend of Lee's at the *Washington Post* had made a collection of all his journalism, and one morning Miranda read some of the work to Lee, in particular some of the more harrowing stories Lee had written from Vietnam and Bangladesh.

After she had finished, she said, "That was pretty great stuff, Dad. You should be proud."

But Lee was angry. "The guy who wrote that couldn't have been there," he said. "I was the only one who was there."

When Lee slept, my stepdaughters and I shared our fatigue and our complaints, and we talked about a future none of us could imagine. Miranda was starting graduate school that fall; Alexandra would begin a new job as a labor organizer. She made her younger sister laugh when she imagined introducing herself to her new colleagues: "Hi, I'm just a big empty hollow ball of sorrow. What's your name?"

Sometimes while the girls stood watch, I would take a walk. I couldn't go to any of the places that meant something to us, so I walked down unfamiliar streets in the East Village. Every now and then I would pass a small piercing parlor, and every now and then I would walk in and get another hole in my ears. I liked the pain; it was as simple as that. I never said anything about it at home. One afternoon I came back to the apartment with a bright red bead sticking out of the top of my still-red ear. Lee looked at me. "If I don't die soon, you're going to end up looking like a Christmas tree."

He began to sleep longer and longer, though occasionally he would wake and his hands would rise and he would try to pluck something out of the air and he would talk to someone who wasn't there. I walked into the room as he was saying in a patient reasonable tone, "I just want to go away with my wife and get away from the cancer. You can't kill me, you know. I'm too young." He saw me looking at him, and he smiled. "I'm talking crazy, aren't I?"

"Not at all."

He saw me watching his arm up in the air, forefinger crooked. "Look," he said. "I'm holding a parrot."

Gently I explained that in fact there was no parrot, and then I saw him smile at me. "I was joking," he said. "I still can, you know."

Lee had stabilized by then. The doctors said that in fact he could live for months. But his clarity was an unpredictable thing.

One afternoon we arrived for a visit and he was alert and very happy to see us.

"How are you?" asked Alexandra.

"I'm very well," said Lee. "But the painting keeps changing."

He was looking at an Impressionist print hanging on the wall. The painting depicted three women standing in a circle on an old stone bridge. "Most people think it's Etruscan in origin," he said. "But it's not. It was painted right after World War II. About an hour ago the plot took a strange turn. I don't know what those women are up to, but I think it's just a postmodernist version of the Albigensian heresy." There followed a loony monologue about an Eritrean puppet show taking place outside his window, and a plot among the nurses to convince him he was gay.

"Where are you?" the doctor asked.

"I'm in a fighter bomber," Lee said.

A few moments later he was quiet, eyes open and unseeing, as if in pantomime of everything that was to come.

"I'm going downhill," he told me the next day. He was quieter, his mind clear. "I don't know what to do. Should I keep fighting, should I keep trying, if I'm dying? But what if I could live longer if I continued to fight on? Then if I give up, I would have made a terrible mistake."

Then you should fight, I said. "For as long as you can. It will be so much better when you come home."

"But I can't do anything," he said. "I can barely move."

"It doesn't matter. Home is where you should be, it's where you want to be. It's where I want you to be."

"Then I would be going home to die?"

I started to cry. Whenever I was faced with the finality of the thing, the grief flooded in, painful and cleansing. I was suddenly faced with the remarkability of the man himself, not what was happening to him, and the tedium and bondage disappeared. All I could think of were the ways I didn't know him and now never would.

After we talked, I read some of the newspapers to him. "I can do this every day, when you get home, and books too. I know it's a little hard for you to read these days."

"Don't leave me," he said suddenly, and I was ashamed of the anger and resentment I felt sometimes, as if he had read my thoughts. "You have no reason to stay. You have everything, and I have nothing to offer."

"I'm afraid you're stuck with me," I said. "Forever and a day."

"And will you stay with me if I make a miraculous recovery?"

"I'll be the one dancing on the rooftops."

A few days later he was home. He sat in his wheelchair in the living room. The hallucinations came and went, and he was proud when he could keep them under control.

"You didn't know, did you?" he asked, as I started chopping vegetables for dinner.

"Know what?"

"About the people dressed in yellow, ushering the others through the revolving doors. You couldn't tell that I saw them?"

"No, I had no idea," I said. "That must be very hard work, separating out what's real and what's not."

"Isn't it always?"

I smiled. "Yes, it is." And then, "I was real. We were real. You know that, right?"

"I knew it before you did."

The nights were very bad. I gave him drugs and painkillers every two hours, but still he was haunted by visions and voices, relentless, pursuing, accusing him of Adrien's death, bringing back battlefields in Vietnam and all the things that happened on them. He wanted desperately to get out of bed to escape the voices, but even so he was patient, waiting for dawn, waiting for me to rescue him. Once during the night I sighed involuntarily as I gave him his medicine. "I should never have come home," he said. "I'm too much trouble." Even with the voices screaming at him, he was trying so hard to make this easy on everyone, to try and keep from us how frightening it was, and it broke my heart. "You have to believe me," I said. "It's so much better when you're here. Like everything is in its proper place. It's about the only thing I'm sure of, that life is better with you in it." I remembered something Lee had said when Adrien lay unconscious, hooked up to the life support systems. Even if it were only this, he said, even if he never wakes up, it would be better than not having him at all, wouldn't it? Please, I thought, if I can just have this, I won't ask for more.

The next morning he seemed restless, writhing and twisting in his wheelchair. I was worried; his bones were so fragile, they could shatter if he fell. "I've been thinking," he said. "There might be a way I can sleep in our bed again." The bed was on a raised platform that involved climbing two steps, and I quailed at the possibility, not only of carrying him up the steps but of the nightmare of urinals and soaked sheets and accidental bumps in the night.

"Why?" I said oafishly. "Why would you want to do that?"

His eyes filled with tears. "So that I can be with you and Zoë again," he said.

I put my arms around his poor wasted body as he tried to clasp his arms around my neck. I pulled him up, the way we did when going from wheelchair to bed, now that he wasn't strong enough to use the wooden bridge. But that had been only a matter of pivoting him into the chair. This time I tried to walk and turn toward the bed with him, he tried to help, and slowly we began to revolve in a circle as if we were dancing, I thought. Exactly as if we were dancing. To have him in my arms again, his beautiful head next to mine, the feel of his body against my body: I drank it in, I wanted it never to end. He was transformed, and I remembered him again, who he was beneath the illness, all the things that had been obscured by the detritus of daily life—his sensitivity, his avid curiosity, his hunger for love so locked away he found it hard to express, his elegance, his lovemaking, his sensuousness, his rigorous sense of decorum and modesty. Holding him, I felt the bedrock of our marriage scoured clean of all its emotional lichen, saw that the reality of the relationship was in the silences, in the fact of our being together, the breathing in and breathing out of it, as regular as the tide.

But I couldn't manage it. I wasn't strong enough to get him to our bed, and I hurt him, and he cried out in pain and I settled him back in the hospital bed. It was the last time he left the bed, but even now I can see it, our last waltz in the morning light, slow and in my mind unending.

The last week he was unable to speak. He communicated with his eyes when he needed a drink, or something for the pain. The days, hot and breathless, passed slowly, and when either Alexandra or Miranda or I had to leave the house, we came back quickly running.

One morning I sat down close to him and began to talk, the words just welling out unplanned. I didn't realize until I began that I was saying goodbye.

"I need to tell you how much I love you," I said. "How much you mean to me, how lucky I was, how lucky we have been, to love each other. Thank you for our time together, thank you for all the happiness you gave me. I will always love you. Please know that I will always miss you, and I know that you will be with me forever."

He listened avidly, drinking in every word, as if it were rain on parched earth. I stroked his great head—he was still so beautiful to look at—and held his hand, and though he couldn't speak, he did move his lips and seemed to strain upward. I realized he was trying to kiss me. I leaned down and kissed him for the last time.

The girls came in, and I left the room so they would have some time alone, because somehow we knew there would be no other time.

By evening his breath was fast and ragged and his pulse was weak and thready. We sat around his bed all evening and held his hand and talked to him quietly. At nine o'clock I put Zoë to bed. No one had eaten much all day, so I put some cold chicken and roasted vegetables on the table, where they sat untouched.

At ten o'clock his breathing became slower and more shallow and then slower still. And then it stopped.

Alexandra took his pulse. She shook her head.

It was 10:36 P.M.

Chapter Thirteen

O NE NIGHT, when he was still a boy, Saint Augustine stole a dozen pears and fed them to the pigs.

As a young man, he would go on to much greater crimes; he spent the whole of his youth in a pronounced pursuit of pleasure. He whored and drank and debauched, he consorted with libertines and dallied with heretics. He was proud, arrogant, ambitious; he was the despair of his mother, Monica, whose tears he ignored but never forgot.

We know all this because Augustine recorded it in his *Confessions*, written long after he had found his God and become a brilliant pillar of the early Christian church. He excoriates himself for all of his wrongdoing in this strange and haunting book, but nothing seemed to have caused him as much pain as the night he stole the pears and fed them to the pigs, when he did wrong simply for the pleasure it gave him: "Such was my heart, God, such was my heart which You had pity on when it was at the very bottom of the abyss."

Augustine had seen himself in a way that he could never escape; it was the moment when he knew himself for the human he was, not the hero he wanted to be, the moment when he was no longer innocent.

That night, those pears, the pigs: they were the lightning that shattered the tree, and Augustine burned and bloomed with it for the rest of his life. I like to think of him that way, an old man in the sun remembering a young thief in the night, a saint trying to understand a sin the size of a pear: *such was my heart.* He couldn't let it go. The moment had too much to teach him. Without it he would not have known himself.

Try not to regret the past too much, wrote Colette, a sinner of a very different sort. It tends to fall away when it is ready, like fruit from a tree.

But the trick, as Augustine discovered, is to catch it when it drops.

Five days after my husband died, I took off my wedding ring. It was the evening after his memorial service, the last of many last things, and our home still resonated with the lingering expressions of sympathy and regret. There was, finally, nothing left to do, and yet I stood in the center of the room, waiting. After what seemed a long while, I realized what it was. I was waiting for the sound of my husband's footsteps coming down the hall. I put the ring back on.

I had a mule and her name was Sal...

I had a farm in Africa . . .

I am the last of all my kind.

All stories are stories of loss, Henry Allen, the best writer I know, once told me.

I looked down at the gold band on my finger and thought about how the act of putting it on ten years before had changed my life. I thought a companion gesture would make real what so far had eluded me. I thought that taking the ring off would make me believe that my husband was dead. What I didn't know was that it would take me a year even to begin to know what that meant.

Grief is a cradle; it can rock you to sleep. I felt a curious nothing after Lee died, not numb or drained, but hidden in a concrete bunker that could keep every emotion out. I knew this place, I had found it when Adrien died. Then I had been afraid it would never crumble, and I would never feel anything again. Now I knew better.

The hospice sent over a sheaf of pamphlets, explaining the mourning process. Grief was a sort of ladder. The first rung was labeled denial. You started there, and then you worked your way through anger and depression until you finally reached the top rung, which was acceptance. They didn't say what happened then. Maybe you got a gold star.

I threw the paper away. This orderly procession did not apply to me. For eleven months I had watched Lee die, I had measured the cost of every moment he lived, I had seen our life together change and my love become funneled into the care I took of him: the sorrow in his eyes was seared into my brain. I had done my grieving, or so I told myself.

Zoë rarely moved more than a few feet away from me in those days. She dutifully filled in the coloring book the hospice sent her—lots of bunnies and squirrels looking sad in the winter and then happy in the spring—and she talked to the grief counselor once a week. But most of the time she played the same computer game over and over and over again: it was called *Jill of the Jungle*, and in it a young woman defeats unimaginable obstacles to rescue an imprisoned prince. Once I overheard her talking to her stuffed animals. *Run, run home quickly*, she said, *before your parents get sick!*

On the first day of first grade she had walked into the classroom with a book about cancer. The book was not written for children; she had found it on my reading pile. She asked the teacher for permission to talk to the class. She read to her classmates a straightforward, no-punches-pulled description of what had happened to her father. Then she shut the book. "Okay," she said. "Any questions? Ask me anything you want now, because after this I'm not going to talk about it again."

For weeks she didn't cry, didn't want to talk about what had happened. But one day she came home in tears. I asked her what had happened. Nothing.

"Then why are you crying?"

"Because there's only one person to say hello to when I

come home," she said. Because no one would ever take his place, because there was no one else in the whole world whose favorite animal was the walrus.

Oh no, I thought as I held her close and comforted her. *I'd forgotten about the walrus.*

I was afraid that Lee was leaving me; the person he had been, the man he was. The real one. In his place was an emaciated saint. I remembered his pain, I remembered his courage, but for a long time I could not remember him alive and happy and healthy. All that I saw was his suffering, all that I could remember were the days of his illness, one by one, and they blotted out everything that had come before.

All that fall I lived like a tenant in the life Lee and I had had together—his shoes still under the bed, his neckties on the closet door, a list on a piece of paper, written in Lee's hand. It was just a list of errands, the kind you scribble as you head out the door: Potatoes. Milk. Olive oil. ATM. Cleaners. I crumpled the list into a ball, and then, horrified at what I'd done, I smoothed it out again and put it in a clean white envelope. Then I took it out and looked at it again, a quotidian piece of a long-forgotten day, the familiar turned foreign, irrevocable and irretrievable.

Even more necessary to me were the ugly reminders of his illness—the red plastic pill container that had kept track of each day's complicated dosage, the wooden plank that bridged his passage from hospital bed to wheelchair, even the beige plastic bedpan. With the artifacts of his illness still in place, I could almost convince myself he wasn't really dead.

One night in September I came home after a day of desperate shopping. My husband's employers had taken away the computer and fax machine we had both used and that I had blithely forgotten did not belong to us. When I got home, I tried to install my new modem into my new computer. The thing wouldn't go in. I tried, desperately, to make it work—my sense of myself as a competent adult, my ability to manage the future, depended on it. The hours went by and the room grew dark. Suddenly there was a loud noise— the coat hooks I had put up on the wall that very afternoon had come crashing down, because, it would turn out later, I hadn't used something called a molly bolt. Zoë screamed and came running. The grief counselor had told me that she was sure something would happen to me when she wasn't around to help. She imagined getting the news and had figured out exactly how long it would take her to walk from her school to the hospital.

At that moment it didn't matter that my husband knew more about Matisse than he did molly bolts or that he would have needed three Bombay martinis before confronting a modem. All that mattered was that I couldn't do these things and I was all there was.

Gradually Zoë and I established a rhythm to the days: the coat rack held, the modem worked (most of the time). I packed up my husband's clothes and put them away. Some memories began to evoke a smile in place of a blast of pain. I would go grocery shopping and walk home in the twilight, thinking about the former importance of cream of sorrel soup and smiling at Lee's stoicism on the nights when dinner consisted of popcorn.

Late in the fall I went back to the beach house he and I had shared since before we were married. It was an unexpected trip—Zoë had left her favorite stuffed animal behind on our last weekend there, and I stole a day in the middle of the week to fetch him.

The errand didn't take long; the scruffy, much-loved object was exactly where I had hoped he would be, left behind on the living room sofa. I tucked him under my arm and headed for the ocean.

The beach was deserted, except for the wreckage of an abandoned plastic chair, the remains of a razor clam, a thicket of seaweed washed up on shore, the usual detritus of summer's end. The water was calm. I walked close to the lapping waves. Just ahead of me a monarch butterfly lay on the sand; its wings fluttered once and then not at all.

Monarchs were always plentiful at that time of year, and Lee and Zoë would go on endless treks, finding the trees in which they gathered, the streets in which they basked in the sun. That memory provoked others, perhaps because Lee and I had not come here together after his diagnosis. At the beach he had always been healthy, and that was the way I suddenly remembered him: how he loved the ocean and hated the sand, the sight of Zoë on his shoulders as he took her into the waves for the first time, his ridiculous yellow swimming trunks strewn with penguins.

"Come back," I yelled, younger suddenly than my daughter. "Come back!"

And something did come back.

As the loss and longing stormed around me, I finally remembered our life together, not the isolated patches of guilt or goodness, but the arc of our own idiosyncratic history: the Valentine towels, the summer I lost him to the New York Mets, the fact that he secretly loved Chet Baker's singing as well as his trumpet playing. Even the times he drove me crazy, the weekends when he would force me through a list of domestic chores when I wanted only to sleep. Together they comprised a marriage, a place that let the air in and kept the rain out.

Epilogue

Eight summers after Lee's death my stepdaughters came to stay at the beach house. This would be the last time we gathered there: these days I crave mountains more than oceans. Miranda and Alexandra had come every year since their father died, first alone, then with their husbands, and now for the first time with their infant sons.

I was up early the morning they were to arrive, making beds and putting away things sharp and small and easily broken.

Finally everything was ready. I sat down and drank my coffee and savored the sunlight flooding the room: it was going to be a beautiful day at the beach. Then I saw it—a circular spot on the carpet. At first I thought it was something I must have missed when I vacuumed, but it was nothing so substantial, just a shadow cast by a largish hole in the screen door that led to the deck.

I'd noticed that hole before, but I hadn't done anything

about it all summer. It was just there, a fact of beach life, like sand on the floor, a small annoyance one had to live with.

But now there were babies coming, and suddenly I imagined regiments of mosquitoes pouring through the opening, bent on devouring tender pink flesh, and I shot out of the chair I was sitting in and ransacked the closet in which the occasional practical item might be found beneath the jigsaw puzzles missing a piece or two and the Scrabble set without the proper number of e's. I found a roll of masking tape and covered the hole with two crossed strips. I sat back down and admired it, my mended screen.

F. Scott Fitzgerald once compared himself during those last sad days in Hollywood to a cracked plate, "the kind that one wonders whether it is worth preserving. . . . It can never again be warmed on the stove or brought out for company, but it will do to hold crackers late at night or to go into the icebox under leftovers." I had always thought I knew how Fitzgerald had felt whenever I reviewed the long list of all the things I had not done, and the even longer catalog of things I probably shouldn't have. But now I wasn't so sure. I liked the beauty of a thing no longer perfect.

Finally the ferry docked, the babies arrived, and the house was in a joyous clamor for the rest of the day. Alexandra's son, Logan, was just nine months old, and he looked up with awe at his eighteen-month-old cousin, who walked sturdily around the house bent on exploration, marching through the kitchen and the bedrooms with impressive courage, until it occurred to the little boy that he was in a place he had never been before. He began to miss his mother and scrunched up his face, readying himself to let out an almighty wail. Miranda, however, saw what was happening, and she called to him, and as soon as he heard her voice, he smiled. And so did we all, I like to think, the living and the dead.

Adrien, she said. I'm here.

Acknowledgments

I used to think of writing as a solitary practice; this book has taught me better. Gratitude and thanks seem paltry tributes to pay in return for the help I received from the following:

Susan Kamil of the Dial Press saw me brilliantly through the blind curves, dead ends, and hairpin turns the project took on its long and winding road.

Flip Brophy, of Sterling Lord Literistic, talked me off many a ledge with wisdom, humor, and unflagging patience.

Cynthia Gorney and Garrett Epps gave unstinting advice and counsel, as well as timely assurances that writing books was rarely fatal.

I am bound to Alexandra and Miranda Lescaze in love and memory, and beholden to them for their lessons in courage.

Bob and Hannah Kaiser and Peter and Susan Osnos provided the warmth and kindness of their friendship and an inestimable link to someone we all hold dear.

And Zoë Eliza Darling Lescaze was then, as she is always, my light, my consolation, my hero, and my love.